# 2012 WRITING FROM INLANDIA

*Work of the Inlandia
Creative Writing Workshops*

AN INLANDIA INSTITUTE PUBLICATION

ISBN 978-0-9839575-2-2

# 2012 Writing from Inlandia
*Work of the Inlandia Creative Writing Workshops*

This publication is the end result of a three-season run of Inlandia Creative Writing Workshops held in four locations: Idyllwild, led by Jean Waggoner & Myra Dutton; Ontario, established by Cati Porter and now led by Charlotte Davidson; Palm Springs, led by Maureen Alsop; and Riverside, led by Ruth Nolan.

The Creative Writing Workshops are part of the Inlandia Institute's Literary Professional Development Program, which also includes seminars on publishing and copyright. The purpose of this core program is to foster creative writing and support the emerging writers of Inland Southern California. The Creative Writing Workshops began in Riverside the summer months of 2008. All of these workshops support the rich literary talent that abides in this creatively vital region.

Workshop participants, many of whose works appear in this collection, are diverse in age, gender, culture, and writing experience. The writing samples here are from those who made it to the finish line with completed stories, essays and poems.

In July of 2010, the Inlandia Institute convened the first official meeting of their Publications Committee, on which I served as Chair. At that time, we had very few policies in place, and it was our job as a committee to set some ground rules for future publications. We designated a manuscript review subcommittee, shared development of the then in-development Inlandia online journal, now fully realized as Inlandia: A Literary Journey, and determined that as the workshops program continued to grow and evolve, so must the signature publication of the workshops program.

In the early stages of Inlandia's creative writing workshops program, founding workshop leader Ruth Nolan spearheaded an effort to reward those in the workshop with publication. Called *Slouching Toward Mt. Rubidoux Manor*, this perfect-bound chapbook with full color cover art was published and distributed to Riverside workshop participants and other interested parties. But as the program grew to include Idyllwild, then Palm Springs, and finally Ontario, it became clear that what was needed was a publication that could encompass all of these workshop participants; something that could be replicated year after year, utilizing the same model, so that there would be a sense of continuity and cohesiveness to the series, so that ten years from now, we could look at back and see the evolution of these writers, who no doubt will go on (and in some cases, have already gone on) to bigger and better publications.

Last year, *2011 Writing from Inlandia,* the combined workshops anthology, debuted at the annual Creative Writing Workshops Showcase reading at Riverside's Back to the Grind coffeehouse.

That afternoon, it sold out.

This year's *2012 Writing From Inlandia* brings you new work by thirty-six talented writers writing in the genres of poetry, fiction, and creative nonfiction. These works represent hours of dedication to the craft, both in the workshop and outside of it.

As Marion Mitchell-Wilson, Executive Director Emerita, once said, "When *Inlandia: A Literary Journey Through California's Inland Empire* was launched in 2006, people asked if that were all; what about the new emerging authors." Yes. What about them? Who was going to nurture and support future generations of Inland Southern California authors? The Inlandia Institute took on that challenge, and has served as a hub for regional writers seeking the support of their peers and the intellectual stimulation of continuing education in their vocation.

This new anthology would not be possible without the hard work and dedication of the many people involved in its production: The Publications Committee members who serve as the Editorial Board: Karen Bradford, Gayle Brandeis, Nikia Chaney, Julianna Cruz, Charlotte Davidson, Larry Eby (Chair), Timothy Green, & Judy Kronenfeld; and of course, the 2012 workshop leaders: Maureen Alsop, Myra Dutton, Ruth Nolan, & Jean Waggoner.

As Inlandia moves into a new phase of growth—Marion Mitchell-Wilson has since retired, and I have moved from acting as the Chair of the Publications Committee to overseeing all of Inlandia's projects as Publications & Programs Coordinator—I am forever grateful to all of Inlandia's writers who, as Marion once said, "...put themselves forward to write about this place and to tell their stories. Thank you for your courage, and for sharing and trusting us with your words."

Writing is hard. Publishing your writing is even harder. Congratulations to all of our workshop participants. Thank you for making your mark on Inlandia.

—Cati Porter, Publications & Programs Coordinator
for the Inlandia Institute

# 2012 WRITING FROM INLANDIA

*Work of the Inlandia
Creative Writing Workshops*

# TABLE OF CONTENTS

# Surveyors of Time

## INLANDIA CREATIVE WRITING WORKSHOP - IDYLLWILD
### LED BY JEAN WAGGONER & MYRA DUTTON

## CONTRIBUTORS

T.S. Bennet, Myra Dutton, Francoise Frigola,
David Calvin Gogerty, Mick Lynch,
Richard M. Mozeleski, T Qi, Joy Sikorski,
Robert B. Smith, Jean Waggoner

## Rain Forest

TOO LATE I SPEAK WITH MANY VOICES

A FEW VOICES OF MONEY AND POWER
LEADING TO MUCH GREED AND DESTRUCTION
AND MANY VOICES OF IGNORANCE
LEADING TO WOBBLING TOWERS OF BABBLE
And what can be done about it?
Nuthin.
Bipedal army ants built a road over the Andes
Using real life Tonka toys
From Pacific port deep into my beloved heart
An artery pulsing with diesel fuel combusted
Slicing at my dirt until the dirty deed was done
So their friends the chainsaw termites
And their friends the helicopter flying beavers
Relieve their friends the World Bunco Maggots
And International Monetary Ferrets
Of their misplaced concern over unpaid debts

Foreign debt could be repudiated like Hitler and Tojo did
But instead of having them kill each other in wars
They put my sons and daughters on board ships like slaves
Pack them in like the ever lesser sardines
My sons and daughters could float on their own but instead
They separate them from their roots and family
Lift them out of their villages using hot air and jet fuel
And float them to their technological islands
Strip off their skins to use as plywood
Render their bones to make furniture
Upon which their new masters sit
While supping on succulent whale meat slaughtered helplessly
After having their eardrums blasted to deafness
Measuring my ocean's temperature uselessly

13

Greater chunks of my meat are missing now
The size of France every five years
I speak from patchwork quilt-lesser cloth
Nobody can come to my aid
I have acquired some deficiencies
I am not immune to feeling loss
While my dwindling jewels are still being plucked from their settings
My few precious crowns are pried from my many mouths
Melted down chopped up reformed
Made into ingots and false idols

Such great chunks of my meat are missing now
I cannot hold my water, I cannot hold my earth
My thinning soil falls out, I pee way out over the ocean
Instead of on Africa where I used to like to pee

After my splendid hardwood erections are pillaged and taken
I am given like chattel to grateful ignorants who burn me
They think they are getting something of value
If they only knew
I feel so useless

They think I am just rocks and dirt
They think I am just plants
They think I am just insects
They think I am just animals
They think I am just air and water
They think I am just electrons spinning around protons and neutrons
They really don't know what to think
They just know they have to think something
They look for a physical grand unification theory
It is right in front of their noses
Any direction they point their noses
It is right in front of them
Can't they smell the stench?
It is not a theory

In that place called America alone
There are 100 million of my poor displaced and inbred cousins
Imprisoned in relocation camps
Strict vegetarians being fed ground up parts of each other
And offal ground up parts from other more wooly cousins
Waiting to have their heads chopped off their muscles sliced

Their organs ground by a race of hairless idiot monkeys
The same hairless idiot monkeys that use the skins
Of the prisoners for shoes coats and branded lampshades with no light
The same hairless idiot monkeys that use their hairy cousins
For experiments opening their brain pans and putting in probes
Dancing around in glee when they press a button
And the hairy cousins jerk and vomit in disgust

They think I am just animals
So they eat me
This is a mistake
I am the progenitor of rocks, dirt, plants, animals, air and water
Atoms and electrons matter and antimatter
I have informed my animal offspring to make themselves sick
When the hairless idiot monkeys put them in concentration camps
To ready them for slaughter they get the jitterbug brain rot
Ollie Ollie Oxen free free free and all fall down
Now they put my sweet innocent cannon fodder
Into ovens in droves and incinerate them
So they wont infect the others with their addled thoughts of rebellion
Briefly reminiscent of memories we are supposed to be ashamed of
Putting them in ovens like cattle
Until the hairless idiot monkeys do the jitterbug and all fall down
Ollie Ollie Ebola-Monkey Free Free Free
Better being quietly euthanized than eaten or experimented with

They think I am just air and water
So they drink me and breathe me
This is a mistake
I have informed the air and water to seek their own level of toxicity
So if hairless idiot monkeys put poisons into air and water

Cancer is all they will get back out

They think I am just plants so they hybridize me
Make it so I cannot have babies
This is a mistake
Make it so the poor farmers that plant me have to beg for seed
From the same hybridizing companies year after year or they starve
Make it so the poor countries have to borrow money
From World Bunco Maggots who direct where to buy the seed
And International Monetary Ferrets who squeal and rub their paws
And direct from whom to buy the chemical poison fertilizer insecticide
They plant us in sameness all together in huge collective camps
Make it so the insects that eat me call all their friends to the feast
It is a celebration of death
They spray me with poison to kill the insects
Then they eat me
This is a mistake

They think I am just insects
They think I am a pest
There is a lot more of me than them
I bite them
I make like a buzz saw in their ears
They try to poison me
There is not enough poison in the Universe to poison me
This is a mistake

They think I am just rocks and dirt
If they have time they think in amazement about abundant life
Springing from just rocks and dirt
But they won't just leave me alone
They mess with me
They think there are things inside of me
They crush me and refine me
They try to psychoanalyze me
Send me to factory schools where they try to make me fit in
The school counselors redefine me as ore
They make me a resource upon which they depend

I have become valuable to them
They have killed many many hairless idiot monkeys over me
To get me, protect me and yell battle profanities in my name
Wherever I am they call me the "land that they love"
They think that they can possess me
This is a mistake

They think I am just electrons spinning around protons and neutrons
They think I am even smaller and name me colors of quarks
I joust with them and their thought
The instant they think I am something I become that
I am willow-the-wisp I am the magician
They begin to think I am metaphysical
I am
They collide one part of me with another part of me and
              I am still me
The hairless idiot monkeys jump around when the collision occurs
They think of a new name for me
They don't have the slightest idea who I am
They [make] me fly apart with my gigantic power and kill for them
So I made them hideous deranged and even more hairless
And skin peel off and fingernails fallout and death was cheap
But death is more expensive now
They try to enslave my power so I can only maim and injure
Bolting antique steam engines together with the Sun
To make power for their hair dryers
This is a mistake

Since they do not love me
They cannot hold me
I am too big for their britches
No suspenders can hold me up
Since they do not love me
They only think of using me and then leaving me
Piercing me gouging me poisoning me damning me
They think of going back to heaven where they think they came from
So they think they act in my name
Some of these hairless idiot monkeys even think they are me

Where do they get the audacity to think that they are everything?
They think I have legs and sit on a throne
They think I have self esteem
This is a mistake
They really don't know what to think
They just know they have to think something

I am not taking this sitting down
I take this spinning around
Twisting and turning on the shishkabob spit
If I turn just right I can throw them off
If I jiggle just a little and take a jog real quick
Whirl like a dervish
Tsunamis will do their work
Oceans will slosh back and forth in their basins
And quickfreeze these unnatural mammoths at the poles
With Big Macs stuffed in their mouths
Humans to me are like a fungus gone awry
Fed too much sugar and fermented
In a darkened dank earthen hallway with tunnel vision.

# Water Child

In the summer, without fail,
my toes and fingers become webbed
and I return to the sea --——
to ancient beginnings, so primordial,
that each molecule once again recalls
the advent of my birth:
its evolution from ocean to land,
its loss of weightlessness and ease.

Every fiber aches for the final plunge
that separates me from heaviness,
that lets me sink back into the womb
of the Great Mother, supported, lulled,
and cradled once more.

Memories of a time, when giant sea creatures
inhabited the world, are coaxed into awareness,
and my body begins to shapeshift.
Muscles never used all year now take form
and stretch, pull, glide, and kick,
spraying water into my nose, eyes, ears, and lungs.

*Yes*, I say to the ever-increasing ability to dive
under the surface and rarely come up for air;
to listen to the clank and shift
of small rocks in the bottom sand,
to witness the pattern of flickering lights:
golds, teals, violets, and aquamarines,
moving in hexagonal and diamond-like shapes,
forming, dissolving, and reforming unendingly,
until I am in a trance
and no longer part of the rabble of man,

I dive deeper still, never wanting to emerge
and revisit lives, dense with gravity and grief.

Here I remain for the duration of summer,
until autumn's cold waters draw me back.
Then - minus tail, flippers, scales, or fins -
hands and feet reconverted, I find the
weighted field condemning me to life on land
until summertide returns again.

FRANÇOISE FRIGOLA

## Tsunami Debris

*At the end of March 2012, an empty Japanese fishing boat that was lost at sea after the 2011 tsunami was found off the coast of British Columbia.*

"Mother, Mother! Daddy is here! Daddy is here!"
"Here he goes again," thought the mother.
Even thousands of miles away from home,
Even on the other side of the Pacific Ocean,
He keeps finding his father.

Again, the mother could not find words
To explain that his father would never come back,
That he was swept away by the tsunami almost a year ago.
How do you explain such a disaster,
Such a loss, to a 5-year-old?

The child kept insisting -
"Mother, I am telling you, this is father.
He even has the gold chain around his neck,
The one you gave him a few days before he went away.
Mother, I am telling you, this IS father!"

Intrigued, the mother rushed to the side of her son.
This time, she did not need to look for words
To explain that the father was gone for good -
Because here he was, on the sand,
Lying in the middle of the filthy debris
That had washed ashore with last night's storm.

"Daddy, Daddy, we are here!" The child was screaming.
"Daddy, Daddy, can you hear me?"

The mother was speechless once more.

Her throat was totally blocked.
Neither tears nor words could come out.

Yes, there was no denying it.
It was, indeed, her husband.
Even though the body was so bloated,
Even though it had been partly eaten,
There was no doubt it was him.

She could only let herself down on the sand.
In an attempt to orient herself,
She started looking around.

In the background, a few hundred yards away,
She saw a boat,
Obviously, a fishing boat;
No one seemed to be on board.
What was it doing there?
By itself, empty of all life?

As she looked further, she realized this was a Japanese boat.
A Japanese boat? By itself? Off the coast of British Columbia?
Like her husband, lying at her feet in the sand?

Nothing made sense!
The world started spinning around her again.
She had no choice; she had to pull herself back.
Her son needed her.
What was she going to tell him?

What memories would her child keep of his father?
What action could she take right now to comfort him,
To diffuse, at least a little bit, the horror of such a discovery?
How could she explain to him that, yes, it was his father,
But he had long been dead.

Then her head started spinning again.
How did he die?

How long did it take him to die?
Did he fight? How long? Did he give up?
What were his last thoughts?
Was he bitten before he died, or, hopefully, afterwards?
Where was he exactly, when the tsunami hit?

For so long she had hoped he was much further inland
And, like her son, that one day, he would reappear.

Now there was no doubt:
He had come back, yes he had,
But not the way she had ever imagined -
Not the way she had wanted.

Would she and her son ever be able to forget,
To at least lessen, this ghastly image
Of his bloated body
With the gold chain
She had ordered especially for him?

# Ode to Spams

Years ago, when I joined the Internet it was advertisement free. It was an unwritten rule, a given that everyone respected — until one day, one person dared… dared to advertise… A lawyer…

From that day on, the Internet changed and evolved.

Now we have the privilege of receiving advertisements in our email!

So many business proposals!
I can become so rich!
I'd better pay attention to these "Urgent Matters."
The process is simple and I will be "of assistance" to an unfortunate Nigerian national, usually the son or the widow of an important cabinet minister who was killed under tragic circumstances. In appreciation, I will get a percentage of the millions of dollars I will help safely transfer to America. All I have to do is first help with the bank fees, then just provide that person free access to my bank account.

I should pay attention and grab this opportunity because, according to other emails, it looks as if I have so many accounts that are overdue!

I am also warned over and over that my "credit status is being 'REVISED,'" that I can "remove all my bad credit" and that my "credit WLL be repaired" Yet, I am also being told that "Now is a good time to refinance" and that my "$5000 credit is approved."

Oh well, if I get into trouble, I can hire "top notch attorneys for pennies a day!"
Wait! There is a better deal: these attorneys can be hired for "pennies a MONTH!"

So many items have already been shipped to me! All I have to do is reply to the email and… give my street address.

I can trade $9.95 for $6,000.
I can refinance my home below 2.25%.

I can order diet pills, Valium, Viagra, Xanax, Ambien, Zoloft, Ativan, and more…on-line. I can even "select the prescription drug of my choice" "from the comfort of my home", and save 70%. Frequently these offers come from Canada. They are not only affordable, but also friendly. These "prescriptions are secure." I am starting to suspect Canada is out to take over the US pharmaceutical industry!

I can buy a digital cable descrambler… legally… of course!

How about "furthering my education on-line" with a "100 percent on-line degree".
That should be easy and fast because I can get a "University diploma THIS WEEK" "without writing ONE TEST"

I feel so popular! So many people, I have never heard of, want to meet me!
How is Sunday for you?
We could meet for coffee?
How about a movie tonight. Call me.
I've missed you so much,

People, on-line, are so polite. I receive so many thank you emails, so appreciative for the information requests I never sent, the free gift I never asked for, and the membership I never applied for.

I can be young again:
In 30 days Guaranteed!
Using "the most effective anti-aging therapy available"
Or I can feel 10 years younger in 10 weeks
I can "Reverse aging and loose weight fast"

For just 8 cents a day, I can end all septic tank problems.

I am even offered
dfghj ovof and dfghj iqb
not to mention these tempting deals… written in Korean alphabet

I am being warned that I "can't stop hair loss once it's too late."

I can "Eat pizza and loose weight"
Or, even better "Eat pizza, watch TV … and lose 22 lbs"?

I can "Get my breast enlarged "
AND
Get: "Magic pills that makes me a bigger man."
These are "All natural penis enlargement pills."

I am being told that
"V*I*A*G*R*A will get it up" (for ½ off!)

And offered to
"Add 2-5 inches. Guaranteed."
"Make it big forever."
"Add 3 inches in only 2 weeks"

This is too much. I tried and tried to resist, but I can no longer do so.
I now have a plan.
I will get "Monster Boobs",
Be a "Man with tools",
Eat pizza AND watch TV to loose weight,
Grow biologically younger,
Definitely give my bank account information to help this poor soul
in Nigeria recover his money,
Be social and answer all these so tempting meeting invitations,
Email my credit card number to get all these free gifts,
Give my social security number and mother's maiden name to get
help to fix my credit while accepting all additional approved credits
and refinancing my mortgage,
Go to this Canadian pharmaceutical website and order "Pure high-

grade coral calcium from Okinawa,"
Spend 8 cents a day to make sure my septic tank works properly,
And, finally, further my on-line education to get a degree in a week.

Oh, I forgot, I also have to order inkjet cartridges: will I choose the
80% off or the 3 for 1 offer?

With a current average of fifty spams a day, and the number growing exponentially, I am starting to have to dig through the spams to
find my emails.

It is said that 30% of our Internet access fees are used to deliver
these spams to our monitor.

Our politicians have decided that doing anything to stop spamming
would infringe on the freedom of speech, therefore would be uncon-
stitutional. The fact is: our politicians do NOT ever see these spams.

Most European countries have taken care of this nuisance. You better not be caught spamming on the other side of the Pond, or you
will pay a hefty fee!

We have to convince our elected officials that this has gone too far. I
have an idea (besides a specialized software). Very easy. We orches-
trate an anti-spam campaign. Starting on an agreed date, we all forward each and every spam to president@whitehouse.gov, and to
everyone in the Senate and House in Washington and in every state
Capitol. Our elected officials may not see the spams, but their staff
will!

And I will make sure to include my favorite spams
"Tired of junk mail?"
"Get rid of spam forever!"

# People of Color

I hate that expression!

It makes me so mad!

I find it SO RACIST!

What it is about: the white skin on one side, and all the other skin colors on the other?

So white skin is the point of reference?

Says who?

When will we learn the concept of "humanity"?

The problem is that we are all participating in this discrimination: both the victims and the perpetrators are responsible, and will be as long as we keep the concept of "people of color."

I have always remembered the first black people I met. Yes, I consciously use the term "black", the term I heard when I was 5 years old. Mr. Sibil was his name. He was a photographer. His daughter, Yamilée, was my age. We played together, and with other children in the village where my family was spending the summer vacation.

One day, Mr. Sibil told, what was for me, the most horrific story. I was only 5 and I still remember my horror, and, especially, my confusion.

Mr. Sibil showed us the palms of his hands and the soles of his feet. To our surprise, they were almost white.

"Do you know why?" he asked.

No one knew, including the adults.

So Mr. Sibil went on to teach us why the palms of the hands and the soles of the feet of black people are always much lighter than the rest of their bodies.

> A long, long time ago, all the people in the world were white. One day, far away in Africa, some of them misbehaved and refused to change their manners. They continued doing their awful things even though God had told them to stop and conduct themselves properly. They were BAD!

> As a result, God became very angry and decided to take action.

> He aligned them naked, standing, with their hand up on a wall. Then, to punish them, He painted their bodies black. In this position, the palms of their hands and the sole of their feet could not be painted and, to this day, remain white.

I was only five, and that story bothered me so much that, to this day, I still remember vividly the story and my feelings. It is only years later that I realized the deep meaning of that legend and the total lack of self-esteem it had instilled in Mr. Sibil.

I can easily imagine a missionary (white, of course) creating such a story...

Anyone who has taken the time to look at human skin darker than the so-called white skin must have seen that it is not plain black, brown, or yellow, or... It is so rich! Especially the black and brown skins!

Just look at the details of the face and, in many cases, you will see all sorts of hues. Teach this to your children: this simple fact could be a starting point of appreciation for the beauty of all human beings.

# DAVID CALVIN GOGERTY

## M'aider

"Mayday, mayday, mayday!" came the distress call over channel 16, the radio guard channel that all vessels monitor while in coastal waters or within radar range of another vessel. It was about 10:00 P.M. on a warm August night. I was navigating a large motor yacht and sharing underway bridge watches with my half-brother Dave, the skipper of the yacht. The yacht had been in San Francisco for the owner to live aboard while he underwent cancer treatments at the Stanford University Medical School. Dave, Loren (the engineer), and I were the only people on board.

We were several miles off the coast of central California, headed south towards Point Arguello, enroute to the yacht's home port in Southern California. There was a steady five-knot breeze from the west, kicking up a slight chop on the surface. The swells from the north provided a gentle following sea. The slight rocking of the boat from the chop made for a very pleasant ride, and as in the old saying, we were "rocking in the cradle of the deep"

Unusually warm coastal waters had allowed an algae bloom, which resulted in the phenomenon known as red tide. In a choppy sea under a full moon, the phosphorescence from the red tide made the surface of the ocean sparkle with light, as if the sea were covered with diamonds. A viewer could easily imagine being in a brightly lit city at night. The effect of all this light was to make the nearby land, or any nearby vessels, totally invisible, because of the bright glitter from the phosphorescence.

The "Mayday, mayday, mayday!" distress call was heard again a few seconds later, followed by the name of the vessel, identifying it as a commercial fishing boat out of Morro Bay, and with the message that one of their crew members had slipped and fallen overboard while retrieving a net. The remaining crew members on the fishing boat dropped their net and commenced searching for the missing crew member.

Dave answered on channel 16, and asked for the fishing boat's

30

course, speed, and bearings to Moro Bay and the light at Point Arguello, which they gave to us. I marked every vessel contact on the radar scope with a grease pencil, while Dave turned the yacht 180 degrees and cut back the throttles, so that we were almost stationary heading due north into the wind. That made it very easy to identify the fishing boat that had lost the crew member. The fishing boat was about 15 nautical miles to the west of us. We turned towards it, increased out speed slightly, turned on our search lights, and began searching. We were unable to see anything because of the bright phosphorescent glitter of the ocean.

Several freighters and other fishing boats also replied to the distress signal, and were headed slowly towards the fishing boat. Because of the phosphorescent glitter, their watch-standers were not able to see anything. The Coast Guard sent out a helicopter from Los Angeles and a cutter from Morro Bay, but their crews couldn't see anything either. Everyone continued searching until the Coast Guard on-scene commander suspended the search from about 3 A.M. until dawn. During daylight, the phosphorescent glitter would be less of a problem.

We resumed our southerly course towards Point Arguello, with enough fuel remaining to get us to our home port. Later the next morning, while in-shore of the Channel Islands, we heard on channel 16 that one of the freighters had found the missing fisherman just after dawn. The fisherman was alive, clinging to a water-logged pallet that had been drifting in the ocean. He was weak, from clinging to the pallet, and slimy from the phosphorescence, but the warm ocean temperature had kept him alive. Although he may have thought so when he went overboard, he did not have his appointment in Samarra that night.

# Help

I was walking down the avenue, when someone handed me a leaflet — a single sheet of paper.
Halfway down the block, I tentatively looked at the paper and began to read.
To my surprise it was simply one word, handwritten, in bold lettering that screamed out to me.
"**HELP!**" it said.
When I turned to see who the fellow was, he was gone.
Had I not reacted quickly enough?
My goodness — I had cash in my pocket. I had plenty to give.
So many had little to nothing. I was certainly ready to contribute.

Help…what a call! It actually gave me a twitch of the divine, but now it was too late. What could I do?

Help, but how? There was much to consider.
Many of us were stuck in our egos … in our need to be right, our desire for success, our fear of losing.
How could I even put a thread of solution into that enormous disconnect?

It was so simple to escape responsibility. It was all so easy to say,
"The problem is too big,
and I am too inconsequential –
too powerless – too easily distracted -
too, too numbified."

"I've got to find this guy," I thought. "I've got to do something."
So I turned around and walked back to the corner where I first saw him,
but he wasn't there—
Too many dark angels, too much separation,
too many human beings that are just plain forgotten.
I looked in doorways, in alleys, around each corner —

32

One block, two blocks, across the street. - - -
but he was nowhere.

My god! Radiation from the Fukushima disaster is, at this very
moment, spreading across the Pacific Ocean.
   Americans live in drug-infested cities — cities, filled with poverty and despair, because major corporations have abandoned the very
places that made them rich.
      Greedy capitalists sing the hymn of the day.
Elections are being bought by billionaires.
   Kids are commercialized to crave crappy junk food, manipulated
all too easily by slick ads.
   Educating our youth has become an option rather than a national
responsibility.
   Even our basic right to affordable health care has been corrupted
by this hymn to the god of profiteering. So much so, a third of our
nation is sick with something that will end their lives prematurely.
Help! HELP! That's it.
This life is about helping.
It's about caring.
It's about finding that man.
Touching that man.
Helping that man.

   Look! There he is!

# Turquoise Afternoon

I wonder what I'm supposed to be
In this enchanted land -
Am I a mold of something else
Or only what I am -
And if I cry when something's lost
Or slips away too soon -
Did you ever watch a raisin flower
On a turquoise afternoon?

The dreaming in this sojourn
Savoring every dream -
Chasing after wanderlust -
Without a scheme to scheme -
A pilgrim from some other time
Trying to get in tune -
Did you ever watch a raisin flower
On a turquoise afternoon?

A friend passed on the other day
An artist through and through -
He's surely gone – and yet remains
'Cause that's what artists do -
But still I mourn, " My friend has left
He's sped away too soon" -
Did you ever watch a raisin flower
On a turquoise afternoon?

One conscious breath revealing
There's a Presence at the core -
The cosmic lights appearing
With their brightening at the door -
And though I tear as beauty fades
This rainbow round the moon -
Did you ever watch a raisin flower
On a turquoise afternoon?

## RICHARD M. MOZELESKI

### Friday Eve

A sweater hanging,
a jacket gazing,
her shoes tapping,
waiting.

Her plants gasping,
the dog's sleeping,
a wine is chilling,
she's been gone the week.

Working briskly
crying silently
she prays constantly.
But now homeward bound.

Breathing easily,
reads contentedly,
sleeping quietly,
smiling peacefully.
She's home.

# Each Day to the Fullest

What is that? I mean, mean REALLY?
A friend lost a friend, unexpectantly.
Life cut short, loss to his loved ones, unnecessarily.
From my friend's mouth, unhesitatingly,
"Goes to show, live each day to the fullest".
What does that mean? I mean, actually?

Is it grab the gusto, have all the fun unregrettably?
Accumulate, consumerate, storageate unrealistically.
Maybe it's check out, check out of it all peacefully,
cause, what you don't know about your neighbor
can't bother you, I mean, seriously.
Or, could it be something, something, something else entirely
possibly in this speck of time we call life.
We should be living eternally.

Eternally?
Yes, eternally.
In this speck of time we call, call life,
this gift from God to us, to use, use so wisedly.
We should re-think what we consider so valueably
to put under His eye, and reconsider carefully
with wisdom, humility and so, so prayerfully
What it means, actually
"to live each day to the fullest".
I say, say so respectfully.

# Idyllwild's Forgotten Men

Walked around people – forgotten men
watch life's bustle, on post office walls.
Their untold stories, of now and then,
sit at peace, unaware of Dow-Jones falls.

Yes – untold stories of forgotten men.
Sorrowful memories – distant families,
given to simple existence,
waiting on God,
waiting on Man.

Walked around people
with such stories to tell.
But like the book un-opened, the book not read,
they sit waiting, for someone to ask
"Who are you?"—"What is your name?"
"Where do you come from?"
"Do you think it will rain?"

Oh, they'll know – you can bet they will.
You see – their home is out there
under some star, atop some hill.

So next time you see that book on the wall,
stop by—say hi—and open the first page.
Yes, it's dusty, and in need of some cleaning.
But when you hear of his story, it will bring new meaning
to "Your" life.

## Time Changes

It's already hot in the sun,
but delightful in the shade.
Now, only sometimes
can you hear the birds swooping,
squirrels scurrying, bees buzzing
or the pine needles fall.
My little neighborhood sounds
more like a small city under construction.
There are new homes being built up close,
huge logging trucks cruising downhill,
ambulance sirens blaring uphill,
firefighting helicopters flying overhead
and underground water rights being loudly lost in our forest.
Now, I hear the din of the chainsaw.
Dust seems to change the feel of a cool breeze.
The usual dry, clean air smells of cut wood crying.
I, too, am saddened for the loss of flora and fauna in these mountains.
Evolution and destruction have their own course.

# Choices

A coyote sauntered
    Down our driveway
        Slowly he went
            Long he stopped
                Looked left
                    And at last
                        Went right

# I Was Kissed By A Bee

I was kissed by a bee
First I said don't kiss me
He flew up from my hips
And landed on my lips
Then crawled all over see
His kiss just set me free
A no tongue stinger
A real humdinger
Please understand my glee
I was kissed by a bee!

# Write It

Pen to the maybe
Open your third eye
You'll never know how
Unless you just try
Let the thoughts come out
And don't question why

# War's Lover

She pulled me to herself, red-hot lips steamy on my ice-blue mouth.
I lay still in the mud, feeling the brown earth pull me deeper into itself.

She laughed and jerked me to her breast, forcing my mouth
over her nipple.
"Drink, you fool, drink.
You will not find your way out of this feast!"

I could not look at her.
Too many memories flooded my eyes with shame.
Too many jagged shards clawed into my nearly beat-less heart.

I drank until a final spasm of my lips broke the suckling hold.

Triumphant in climax, she shrieked at the sun, her voice
like a small black dot
circling into the light with an eclipse of sound
that grew and expanded until it shut out all voices.

As I slumped to the ground, she rose victorious and flew to a
trench on the opposite side of the field, leaving me to rot
where I had fallen.

The last sound I heard before closing my eyes forever was her
screaming at the man I had shot six seconds before she
had kissed me.

"Drink, you fool, drink.
You will not find your way out of this feast!"

## A Wilderness Next Door

When I think of the San Jacinto Mountains, the word "isolation" comes to mind.

This may seem an odd association. Their highest peak stands but seven miles west of the desert resorts of Palm Springs, barely ten miles south of the Morongo Casino in wind-blown San Gorgonio Pass, two attractions linked by congested interstate freeway. Only thirteen miles to the southwest are the citrus groves bordering the town of Hemet. Even the smog-belching hub of the urban Inland Empire lies a mere three-dozen miles to the northwest. It's hard to exaggerate how small a footprint this tree-clad island of granite occupies amid the sere hills and valleys encircling it.

Yet experience has taught me that these mountains are indeed isolated. It's less a question of geography than of topography, biology, and culture. The San Jacintos' singularly vertical profile demands miles of twisting roadway or trail to gain access. Conditions ranging from low desert to subalpine forest cloak their slopes. The higher I ascend, first by car, then on foot, the more puny seem the human artifacts strewn across landscapes far below. Once engulfed in oak and pine groves on the coastal face or pinyon and ribbonwood stands on the desert side, Southern California's freeways, housing tracts, and strip malls simply fade from consciousness.

This passage from valley floor to mountain heights requires acclimation of body and mind. Attempted shortcuts are misguided. The Palm Springs Aerial Tramway, with all the charm of a crowded amusement park, plucks riders from suburban desert heat and drops them moments later onto the chilly rim of boulder-strewn forest totally unlike the environment they left behind. It's no wonder rescue teams must be habitually summoned to save the unprepared and disoriented from fatal misadventure. The isolation of the San Jacinto Mountains is something to embrace, not subvert; to celebrate, not deny.

As the last high mountain range short of the Mexican border, the San Jacintos did once enjoy a measure of geographic distance from Southern California's metropolitan heart. That protection from hordes of weekend and holiday escapees vanished when the day-long journey from Los Angeles shriveled to a couple of hours, and the post-war population explosion pushed the perimeter of settlement into valleys at the foot of the range. Yet even today, solitude remains close at hand.

Admittedly, I learned this lesson from a privileged position. My supreme stroke of luck in life was being born during the Depression to parents who had forsaken the luxuries of their upbringing for the frugal life of the Protestant clergy. As I was growing up, they could ill afford vacation travel. Instead, for as long as a month each summer we took advantage of free lodging at my grandparents' primitive retreat, tucked away in a tree-covered valley 6,000 feet up in the San Jacintos.

When I was first brought here in 1939, the long drive from Los Angeles climaxed in 25 jolting miles of dirt road. Even with Highway 243 now paved, three miles of dirt and a locked gate still buffer our refuge. Ringed by jagged peaks and steep wilderness ridges, its remoteness has forestalled intrusion by pavement, power lines, sidewalks, street lights, sewers or other seeming necessities of modern American infrastructure.

Isolation was the bait that lured me back to this spot, summer after summer. My first sensation on arrival, after months amid the cacophony of urban life and hours of highway noise, was sheer silence. Soon my ears would gradually attune to a more subtle sound, the rise and fall of a gentle wind in the pines, now high in the treetops, now swooping to ground level. Against this backdrop John Cheever once called the "endless noise of passing silk," I would begin to register distinct reports—the hammering of a woodpecker in the oak overhead; the screech of a Steller's jay in the creek bed nearby; the croak of a lone raven gliding over the apple orchard; assorted cheeps, twitters, and trills from songbirds on wing or limb; the chatter of a gray squirrel mining a pine cone; the buzz of hovering gnats seeking entry to eyes, ears, nose, or mouth; the thudlet of a falling acorn striking the dirt beside me. In quieter moments, the faint rumble of a distant waterfall added a relaxing note.

My wristwatch would quickly find its way into a drawer, freeing me to live for a month, a week, or a weekend at nature's pace. The

44

diurnal rhythm of the forest admitted only three distinct moments in time each day—sunrise over Fuller Ridge, sunset over Black Mountain, and midday, which I detected using a natural sundial, the shadow of one particular Jeffrey pine's trunk precisely covering the trunk of its neighboring sugar pine. Each night as I was falling asleep I lay peering through tall firs and pines that stood like colossal paint-brushes reaching up to tint the star-speckled sky, where passing con-stellations dot the face of another natural clock.

We did have a cabin beside Fuller Mill Creek, a decrepit relic from an 1878 sawmill. But we passed our days on a nearby shelf formed from a decomposing granite outcrop, shaded by oak, pine, cedar and fir, within earshot of the creek. Here four generations cooked, ate, drank, relaxed, read, conversed, and entertained them-selves as the spirit moved. Our furnishings were minimal: a home-made picnic table; a fragment of an earlier table serving as a kitchen workstation; shelving anchored to a sugar pine for canned goods and utensils; air-tight, thirty-gallon shortening cans for foods susceptible to dehydration or animal pilferage; a nondescript collection of canvas director's chairs; a hammock slung between two pines. The back seat from an ancient Dodge sat before the campfire ring, itself once the sawmill blacksmith's forge. Rounding out the infrastructure were a single faucet delivering icy water piped by gravity from a spring and a huge, flat-topped, wood-burning cookstove made of local granite.

In this place that offered "nothing to do" by today's adoles-cent standards, I spent my days exploring trails, trees, and rockpiles, playing games, swimming in the creek, observing animal behavior, or settling into the hammock with a paperback cowboy novel. Intimate contact with nature became absorbed into my being as a conglomera-tion of sights, sounds, and smells instantly retrievable from memory. The silver sheen of moonlight on pine needles, the vivid green of a healthy fir framed by deep-blue noonday sky, the buzzing choir of bees among chinquapin blossoms exuding an aroma already well along towards honey, the scent of pine duff baking under the after-noon sun, the perfume of azalea blossoms lining the creek, the residue of cedar campfire smoke clinging for days to a sweatshirt—these remain my landmarks of home.

Today, I dwell year-round in the San Jacinto Mountains' sole village, Idyllwild. A weekend resort, it fills with tourists every seven days like clockwork. But its residents have sustained a community culture unlike that of crowded Southern California. The pervasive sense of isolation is still only minutes away. Trails leading out of town whisk me into ravines and valleys insulated from the clatter of civilization. Nearby vista points reveal forest uninterrupted by signs of human occupation. And a twenty-minute drive returns me to my true home in the woods, where the calming hand of solitude isolates me from the cares of the day and restores peace of mind.

Attraction to forest is in our genes, an impulse shaped by eons of life in such a setting, long before evolving human culture imprisoned us in artificial shelter. What the isolation of the San Jacintos offers, above all else, is restoration of the ancient affinity between people and nature.

There is magic in these mountains. Spend time apart from the distractions of civilization, and it will find you.

# Jean Waggoner

## Desert Candle
### [*Caulanthus inflatus*]

The RV was hot and Ashley was bored. Mommy kept saying, "Go outside and play with your brother," but Reggie and his friends never played anything fun. Clem wouldn't let her sit on his lap. "It's too hot," he said. The T.V. was broke; Mommy and Clem both said so. Ashley tried to turn it on, anyway.

"Go outside! We got work to do!" yelled Mommy.

"Yeah, get lost!" said Clem.

Ashley went to get some toys, but most of the Barbies and Power Rangers and Transformers didn't have all their legs and arms, or their heads were off. The teddy bear and the Barney smelled bad, like maybe cat pee, and anyway, she was too old for Barney and that old stuffed bear that used to be her grandmother's. She was six now.

"You hear your mom? We got mixin' to do, " said Clem, "Time to go out!" It was hotter than the RV outside in the desert. Ashley didn't want to go. "Can't I stay? Can't you read me a story? Can't I sit here and Clem play me a song on his guitar?"

"No!" Mommy yelled from the sink.

"Can I have a popsicle, then?" Ashley asked.

"No!" answered Clem.

"When you come back," Mommy promised, "Stay out for an hour."

"A whole hour! What can I do?" She didn't want to go outside.

"Play with your brother." "Go!" the adults ordered.

"OK, just let me get – " Ashley was tired of having to leave and go nowhere, do nothing. She ran back to the room to get her purple purse and her secret Kleenex that was all folded up around her five dollars from Uncle Joey with his phone number on a piece of paper. Maybe she would run away this time. Maybe Uncle Joey would let her stay with him.

She went out the door, down the metal steps with the fake grass on the first one and the piece of her grandmother's old green

47

carpet on the next one and stepped onto the crunchy ground. There was a lot of crumbly rock out here on the Mojave. Most of it was black and white, but it was mixed with sand and dirt of different colors. Sometimes Ashley could find a piece of quartz, a kind of white, glassy rock, if she looked for it.

This time she was looking for her brother Reggie. It wasn't hard to find him. All the lots were flat. There were no trees and only a few of the lots had RVs or vans or trailers on them. In fact, Reggie was over by Joel's folks' RV with Joel and Wade.

"What's up?" called Joel, all happy, but Ashley didn't want to play with the boys. "Nothin' " she answered and kept walking. Reggie and Joel and Wade had a can of old oil, drained from Clem's car. They were pouring the oil on anthills and putting them on fire with kitchen matches. It smelled smoky, like the big trucks out on the highway. The oil smell wasn't as bad as the burnt toilet cleanser smell in the RV when Mommy and Clem were mixin' stuff, but it smelled dirty and it made the air hotter. It was still in the school year, not summer, but it was a pretty hot afternoon.

"You sure you all right?" asked Joel. "Sure," she told him and walked on. She could hear the boys' mom goin' *click, click* with her tongue at the top of her mouth and gripin' to Wade and Joel's dad, "Them sendin' the girl out to amuse herself all afternoon with no young girls in the neighborhood…" and she knew Joel's dad, retired from over at the air base, would be sayin' back, "At least she ain't in there breathin' that foul air. One a them oughta get a job. It's no way to live."

"An old bag in dirty sweats" was what Mommy called Joel's mom. Mommy wore good jeans and pretty tops and wasn't fat. Ashley wanted to be with mommy – or at least to find something pretty to look at. At their old house there were trees and flowers and a swimmin' pool and nice chairs. The house was big, too. Ashley missed her own room where she had a pink bedspread and her good dolls and toys. Mostly, she missed Daddy. She wanted to go back to the old house, but Mommy said it was sold. Mommy said Daddy was sick, and anyway, he wasn't sendin' money.

"Daddy!" she cried, almost out loud. Nothing was pretty here. It was all just crunchy dirt and a bunch of weeds that didn't even look like weeds 'cuz they were so dried up. Ashley wasn't sure if she could walk to town, or what she would do if she got there, but she got out on the road. It was made of red crunchy dirt with a kind of orange crust and it smelled oily.

She walked for a while and then some boys came by ridin' fast on dirt bikes yellin' "Beep! Beep!" She moved over to the side of the road and started walkin' faster. It was really hot out and she started gettin' sweaty, but she found that if she slowed down just a little the sweat dried up – or maybe it even stopped. She wasn't sure which, but she quit havin' to wipe her forehead with the back of her arm, if she walked at just the right speed.

Pretty soon, the road started to go up – just a little, but she was walkin' uphill. It made her pant, all out of breath. After awhile, though, she could look down and see somethin' besides just the road and empty lots. Was it a house? Mommy and Clem hardly ever took her to town with them, and even if they did, it was usually after dark, maybe to catch a movie and go shoppin' over at Victorville. She wasn't sure which way to walk to find town or even a 7-11. She wished she could see a real house again, just to sit and look at it.

"I wouldn't bother nobody – I mean *anybody*," she said to herself, remembering her grandmother's English corrections. Mommy never wanted her to bother the people who lived in houses. Since they moved here, they didn't know any people who lived in houses, only people in RVs and vans or cars on the lots and some other people who came to the RV at night after she and Reggie were in bed.

It looked like a real house way down the road, for sure. She started walkin' faster, toward it. She didn't hardly notice her feet on the road, or how the sun was movin' toward the way-off hills. She got on a beat like in her old dance class: step, step – skip – step; step, step — step & — turn, but she didn't skip or turn very big 'cuz that took a lot of happiness; she just paced along soft-like, thinkin' about bein' in dance class, her life before…step, step, skip — then, suddenly, she fell! Her hands hit the crunchy ground first, then her knees, kind of sideways, then her elbows, then her butt, and then the side of her head.

"Owww!" she cried, to nobody. "Ooww!" There wasn't anybody to cry to.

There was nothin' to do but to sit back and brush herself off and look to see if she was cut anywhere. Her right hand and knee were pretty scraped up and she had to pick little pieces of rock out of her skin. Her mouth was almost totally dry, too, but she began to lick the inside of her hand. It started to bleed and pretty soon it was a red muddy, bloody mess. Still, the blood didn't run too much, so she decided to spit on her fingers and wipe her knee.

Her knee hurt. She hurt ever'where. Would her hand be O.K.? Would her knee? Who would help her?

"Ooooh!" she cried! She wrapped her arms around her legs and rocked back and forth, crying, "Ooooh! Oooooh!" She wished Mommy would come to help her.

After a little while, she got quiet. She should think. What should she do? Rest for a minute….decide…? How long had she been sittin' there? She wasn't sure. She'd wait a bit.

She was just startin' to feel normal again when she noticed somethin' really different. Right there, next to her, beside the road was somethin' really pretty! It was weird, like lots a stuff on the desert, but yes, it was pretty – a weed? – a cactus? – a flower? Weeds weren't really pretty and cactuses, like the one on Joel 'n' Wade's mom's counter, were prickly.

This looked like it could be prickly. It had a fat stem with prickly-looking things at the bottom, near where the leaves came out. It had skinny leaves. They weren't too green, but the stem was bright green like glow-in-the-dark plastic Jesus green. The best thing was the tiny flower at the top! Really and truly, it was a flower – a dark, pur-ply flower, a teeny little one, but a real flower – a dark, purple flower on a glow-in-the-dark flower stem! It reminded her, in a odd kinda way, of the candles her grandmother lit at Easter time, so far away and really beautiful.

"Wow!" she said aloud, "Wow! Would ya look at that?"

She got a little closer. Har grandmother liked flowers and had a lot of them in her garden – not out here in the desert, but where peo-ple had lawns. Ashley would have to ask her grandmother the name of this one. She looked some more. At their old house she liked to pick flowers for Mommy and take them inside. Sometimes, though, Mommy wasn't happy when she did that.

Ashley started to reach out, but her hand stopped. Somethin' wasn't right. Only four or five tiny flowers were here. The stems seemed to be lit up like magic. They were so weird! Maybe they were poison! Maybe she should leave them here. Should she? She couldn't decide, so she sat there lookin' just a little longer. They were really pretty, but they made her feel sad, too.

"Beep! Beep!" She sat up, surprised. It was the same boys on the dirt bikes again, goin' the other way. What if they hadna seen her? She might have been hit. Would they try to hurt her on purpose? She started to feel afraid, but then she noticed that one of them looked like Wade's friend from middle school.

"It's gittin' late," he said, " 'Better git on home!" He was right. The sky was gettin' dark. Kids shouldn't be out alone. How far was it to home? Was it an hour yet, an hour since she went outside? Could she go back and sit in her and Reggie's room?

Ashley shivered. It wasn't cold; she just felt somethin' strange. Did she breathe somethin' odd, sittin' by those glow-in-the-dark green and purple flowers? Could she be poisoned? She got back on the crusty road and walked fast. She needed to get home to Mommy and get her hand and knee cleaned up.

Then suddenly, she heard "KABOOM!"

A huge firecracker went off, way off down the road, the way the boys went. She could hardly see where she was headin' to, except that she hurried toward the light. Who was settin' off fireworks? It wasn't the Fourth of July yet! It wasn't even summer.

"KABOOM!" Again, it went off, and ever'thin' got light. A big stick of fire with all kinds of colors in it went up into the night. It had red, yellow, orange, blue, green, purple… green, purple….green and purple, like the flower, in it.

"KABOOM!" It looked like an RV.– like her RV, where she had left Mommy and Clem. More fireworks came. Oh no! Ashley could see smoke and fire goin' up. "OH, NO!" she ran, yelling.

"Mommieeeeee! Mommieeeeee!"

# Distances and Angles

INLANDIA CREATIVE WRITING WORKSHOP - ONTARIO
LED BY CATI PORTER

## CONTRIBUTORS

Jennifer L. Bielman, Larry J. Dunlap,
Marie Griffiths, Krystal B. Moon, Linda Rhoades,
Kelly Smith, Marsha Schuh, Kathryn Wilkens,
Janis Young

# JENNIFER L. BIELMAN

## Horned Melon

We had been there before. A secret garden, a place so few knew about. So secluded no one could ever hear me—us. It was a retreat from our lives, to forget the past. To talk, laugh, heal.

The soft grass tickled my sensitive flesh as I lay back on my elbows. The bright sun had risen only a few hours ago. It felt warm, inviting, as if the rays were open arms, offering safety.

I could feel him close to me. He was always within touching distance. He needed to know that he could reach over any time and I would still be there.

He was just starting to assemble our assortment of fruit. The horned melon was the wild card. It was an adventure for both of us. The unknown made me nervous. The anticipation was always the worst.

The small melon fit perfectly in his hands as he pulled it out of the basket. With it no longer being able to hide in its dark home, I could see its beauty for what it was. He set it on the plate, and I examined the exotic fruit. The yellow specks resembled floating leaves in a burnt orange river. The mini volcano spikes scattered on the skin made it impossible to handle without injury.

He grabbed the fruit, preparing to cut it, when he yanked his hand back and swore. I flinched. The silence was heavy as he nursed his hand. Then he laughed. "A melon with defenses," he said. I put a smile on my face because I had to.

Giving it another try, he ripped into the rich fruit without thought of the damage it caused him or the melon. It seeped dirty white seeds among lime green jelly. A bouquet of unripe pumpkin and grass hit me. The thick goo ran between his fingers, streaming down his arms like blood. I closed my eyes, not wanting to watch the fruit bleed. Laid open like it was weak and in need of help.

He grabbed my hand. His callused fingers abraded my softer skin. Instinct had me pulling away. He held on tight, smirking as he placed the demolished half of the fruit in my hand. The horns cut into my palm, making my eyes water.

Why must a melon have defenses? Why does its unique beauty have to be tarnished for one's pleasure, to quench one's hunger? I looked into my husband's eyes and knew why.

# LARRY J. DUNLAP

## The Nook at Caesars Palace

Excerpted and condensed from
*LOOK BACK IN LOVE, My Life as A Naked Car Thief*

Jesus Christ! That's Debbie Reynolds pulling on Dave's leg!

"Sing it, baby, sing it!" the movie star screamed, grinning up at Dave. Dave was bracing himself to hit the big note near the end of "I've Got You Under My Skin" when she appeared below the edge of the stage. As Dave's rich tenor swept up into his powerful full-voice range and then higher yet into a dramatic falsetto run, she reached up and tugged on the only part of him she could reach, his left pants leg just above a white patent leather boot. She shook it like a rag doll in encouragement.

Dave had to be astonished but he closed his eyes, leaned back and let his golden pipes go. Nothing could surprise us tonight. It was December 1966 and we were on the bill opening 'Nero's Nook,' a mini-showroom holding 250 or more people in 5 tiers of tables inside Caesars Palace. Beyond the bright stage lights everything was dimly silhouetted, cigarette lighters, lit like fitful fireflies haloed in cigarette smoke. We didn't have to see the room to know it was crammed beyond capacity, or to feed on the electrifying connection between performers and audience.

"I've got you . . . " Dave crooned into the final phrase, the movie star still hanging on to his pants leg and smiling up at him. I glanced over at Mac, eyes wide, as we built our final harmonies, "Never win, never win . . .," the entire lounge erupted for another standing ovation in this set with yells and excited screams carrying over the thundering applause. More people rushed down in front of us.

I looked across the stage where we were in our three-lead-singer configuration, we were in a zone, like a basketball shooter gets when he knows he can't miss. Jackets from our shiny, deep ocean blue suits lay rumpled across the stage. Matching sun yellow and white polka-dotted ties lay askew or strewn. Azure cuff links on custom tailored white-on-white dress shirts sparkled in the stage lights. We might be called Stark Naked and the Car Thieves but we dressed to the hilt when we hit the stage.

I glanced at Leonard as I slipped behind my Hammond B3. He was sopping wet, his shirt translucent; he grinned like an escaped maniac, clicked his sticks and we jumped into an R&B set closer, "Can't Turn You Loose," as the curtain began to ring down.

We'd tried to close the set twice before but the crowd kept drawing us into another song, another tempting hit from the ultimate, irresistible narcotic, an adoring audience.

An hour earlier, before we started the set, I'd peeked through the curtain. "Son of a bitch, you guys, I see Joey Bishop and Peter Lawford and I think I see . . . Omigod, it is, it's Sammy Davis!"

"Could Frank be out there?" whispered Dave behind me. "It would be ultimate."

"I saw Lou Rawls sittin' with Johnny Mathis and the Cos is out there, too." Mac grinned. Johnnie Mathis was closing in the main showroom tonight, he'd been in almost every night this week, and it was great to see Bill Cosby out there. He often crossed the street between shows at the Frontier to hang out with us at the Cat.

Somebody behind me said Diana Ross was in the audience and Leonard said Don Rickles was at somebody's table. We were in the second weekend of the room's opening and it was getting around town that there was something big happening at the Nook. We'd counted at least twenty-two stars out there before we took our places to start the set. I'd thought my heart was going to explode when the curtain started to rise.

Now, after the descending curtain gradually muffled out shouts, whistles and frenzied clapping, the silence on the darkened stage was deafening. None of us said anything. We held on to that transcendent moment where nothing mattered except the performance for as long as we could, nobody wanted to break the spell.

There would be a price to pay for tonight but I wasn't ready to think about it yet. We'd played to some great audiences, had our share of standing ovations and cheering but we had just played for celebrities from the biggest league in the entertainment business—beyond our peers—and damn, they'd loved us. We'd let it all hang out for the first time at Caesars. I looked at us, wrung out, sweat dripping.

I was so proud of our band tonight.

Les said something then that I will remember for as long as I remember this night.

"What?" I said, stepping down from behind the B3, not quite hearing him over the muted roar in my abused ears.

"We've finally made it," he repeated louder as he slipped off his guitar strap, "to the top of the bottom."

"That's a hell of a thing to say, Bear." I knew he meant that for bars and clubs, this was everything you could ever want as a performer. But our goal had always been hit records, and concert tours. Somehow though, our success in night club performing had brought us here.

"Yeah, I get that; but why such a buzz-kill now? We should be feeling great after a hot set like this."

"Didn't want us to forget what we really want," he said, turning away.

Not everyone loved us. Xavier Cugat stepped out of the backstage shadow and hissed at me, "You hijos de puta ran fifteen minutes over!" Charo gave me an enigmatic frown as she glided past but I couldn't tell if it was for me or the famous band leader.

"Sorry," I said. I meant it but I couldn't bring myself to regret it.

"You have not heard the end of this, senor. I am the headliner por Dios!" he hissed over his shoulder as he brushed past me in anger.

I had barely registered Cugat's venom when Clyde's face popped up in front of me. He was our supposed personal manager. "Fucker!" he blurted out. "Fuckers! What the hell did you do out there? What are you guys thinking? We agreed. Dave V is going to be fucking pissed. Assholes!" he said, before stalking away. My stomach churned from getting jumped like that. Well, I knew things would happen after our decision in the dressing room before we came down to the stage.

Two Maitre d's were back stage with invitations. One was from Sammy Davis, Jr.'s table. That was especially cool for me since I'd recently read and admired his book, *Yes I Can*, even buying individual copies for the band. Now I was getting to meet the man. The other invitation was for Dave, a personal request to join Debbie

Reynolds and her husband at their table. Leonard was already on his way to see Cosby.

The house lights were up as we wedged our way through the still crowded room and the heady smell of cigarette smoke, perfume, booze and celebrity. The room buzzed with voices and light laughter as Mac and I smiled and waved, acknowledging people I had only seen on a screen or stage before. Less than two years before in Indianapolis, my life was in tatters, the band broken up, marriage exploding, building record players on an RCA assembly line; how could I have ever guessed where we'd be or who we'd be performing for now.

"Hey guys," Sammy stood for us, and lit up that famous megawatt smile. A rich red tie and stickpin, stylishly askew, fell across a high-collared white-on-brilliant-white dress shirt and low-cut brocaded vest; matching blood red cufflinks peeked out of his dark velvety jacket's cuffs.

"You know you guys put on a great show, man. Love the voices, love the energy. This is what rock music is all about, right?" Sammy said. Mac and I both said thanks as we were invited to sit.

Sammy said, "Sonny here . . .," waving a hand full of rings toward two empty chairs where Sonny Charles had apparently been sitting, " . . . well, Sonny when he was here, tells me you guys are really called Stark Naked and the Car Thieves. Love it. Heard of you, killing it at the Pussycat A GoGo club, right? That's crazy, man. Love that." His animated charisma was dazzling.

"So what's with the name change? Big Spenders? What's that?" He took a drag off his cigarette and answered his own question. "Oh, I get it. Hotel don't like "Stark Naked" up there in 6 foot letters, right?" he nodded, exhaled and crushed his smoke out. "God damn these hotels, man. Sometimes they just don't get it." Mac and I nodded vigorously.

"Where is your band from, man, where's home?" he asked, shaking out a Camel filter and offering the pack to us. He tilted his head a bit to the left to keep us in his good eye. Mac took one and a light from Sammy's lighter.

"Most of us are from the Midwest originally but now L.A.," I said. This was so unimaginable; Sammy wanted to know about us. These last several months had been incredible. What was I saying, these last two years.

"Good." He inhaled and let it out, "Me, I'm going back home to LA after we close next week. Maybe we can get together down there. I'd like to help you guys. Talent like yours needs to be seen and heard. What do you think?"

"That would be so cool, man!" Mac said. We looked at each other's huge grins.

I told him how much his book and life story meant to me, how it was inspiring the band. At least I hoped it would, I amended silently. Sammy nodded graciously and leaned forward. "I got to get back to the Sands for my last show. Say man, why don't you bring your guys over to my show tomorrow night. You're dark here, right? We can fit in some time together between shows. " He snuffed out his cigarette and stood up. "Come back to my dressing room before the show, you wanta do that?"

Guys straggled back into the dressing room to shed their wet and wrinkly clothes. We wouldn't be wearing those for another set. Leonard was collecting every suit, tie and dress handkerchief, cuff link and boot. His offstage gig was 'laundry," keeping our outfits cleaned and organized for each show.

"Cosby says we sounded better at the Cat," Leonard said, as he snatched up another pair of pants. We didn't have to worry about losing keys or change, our suits fit like body gloves. The coats had faux pockets and the pants, no pockets at all, even zipping up on the side; John Lieu, Liberace's tailor, had made them for us and they were surprisingly comfortable and easy to move in.

"He also said I needed more drum lessons," Leonard chuckled. "He really liked us tonight."

Dave walked into the dressing room, coat and tie draped over his arm.

Our dressing room was large as you'd expect at Caesars but outside of the deep pile carpet, there weren't many frills, it was more like a locker room then a dressing room for performers. A plain row of tall lockers sat along one wall and a well-lit row of mirrors along another with entry into a shower room with toilets through another. The last wall held an eclectic mix of upholstered and folding chairs.

"So tell us about Debbie Reynolds and . . . what is her husband's name?" I asked Dave.

"That was so cool, man, her hanging on your leg like that. What'd she say about that?" asked Mac.

"Her husband's name is Harry. They're both great. They just thought we were great, that's all." He grinned. "And she, Debbie, was really sweet; she said I 'sang my ass off.' Said she had to run up and grab something and push me to sing harder. Hah!"

"I'm just glad you didn't accidentally kick her in the face," Les said. "I can see the headlines now. 'Singer kicks movie star in Nero's Nook.'"

"You know," I said as I got everyone's attention now that we were all here. "Clyde grabbed me as we were leaving the stage. He called me everything but a 'nice guy' before stomping off. He says Dave Victorson is going to be pissed."

Nobody said anything. Dave Victorson was the Entertainment Director for Caesar's and emperor of all the talent at the hotel.

Clyde Carson had come to us a few weeks ago at the Pussycat A GoGo. The "Cat" was in back of a race book and liquor store on the Las Vegas strip tucked between the Sands and the Thunderbird. It turned into the hippest, hottest rock 'n roll dance club in Vegas as day turned to night. There was always action in the hot and crowded rooms after dark, but it really got going after the big shows closed. We were having a great run there, with lines outside and bouncers enforcing a waiting list at the door.

Clyde was a slight, nondescript, pasty-faced guy with a mustache so thin it looked like it was painted on. He made the completely unbelievable pitch that he could get us an audition to open the rumored new lounge across the street at Caesar's Palace. Ridiculous—Caesar's was more than just across the street; it was across the entertainment universe for a band like us. No major hotel had ever let a rock band play in any of their rooms. Let alone Jay Sarno's incredible resort, Caesar's Palace. At more than twice the size of any other hotel in Las Vegas, Caesars was a gigantic step up in luxurious Las Vegas hotels when it opened last year. Its legendary glamour and opulence overshadowed everything built before it. We might be popular locally but Caesar's was internationally famous. We were like a hot Little League team being asked to audition for Major League Baseball.

But as crazy as it sounded, we got an audition and nailed it. But a few small changes: we couldn't use our name, had to perform only our big vocal harmony tunes, no rock or R&B, and we were following our old Indiana nemesis, The Checkmates, Ltd. And oh, Clyde would get to be our personal manager if we got the gig. We'd accepted those points but they grated on us more than we'd realized over the first two weeks at Nero's Nook—especially giving up two thirds of our repertoire, crippling our ability to compete with the Checkmates.

So that's why, at a hastily called meeting before we got dressed to go on stage that second Saturday night, at the biggest engagement in our career so far, the guys had called me out.

"Larry," Dave started, "We're getting screwed. The Checks are lighting the place up and not only are we getting the ass end of the schedule, we can't compete without our whole song list."

"It really sucks, man," chimed in Leonard. "I feel like I should play with brushes. I don't mind using brushes but, you know, we're not that kind of band. We gotta rock." Craig was shaking his head in agreement. Leonard used small tree trunks for drumsticks so I didn't buy the brushes bit but I understood his complaint.

"We have two early sets that are like dinner shows, and we have to do quiet stuff for those, I see that," Leonard continued. "We've only got one decent show time at 11:00 but it always follows the Checks and maybe they are an R&B band but they also play rock. And we can't; we don't have all our tunes, Larry." Leonard actually moaned. "To be good too, we need all our tunes."

"I get it guys, I do," I said. "We're the bottom act of six on the bill, so of course our schedule's the worst." I knew it would be tough when I signed the contract. I wasn't sure we could do it. But I didn't realize how hard it would be listen to the crowd going nuts for Sweet Louie and Bobby and Sonny while we had to follow them with easy-listening tunes when the room wanted to rock. I shook my head in frustration. "The Checkmates are great entertainers but I know we can play with those guys. The bottom line, though, is we agreed to the contract terms."

"No we didn't, you're the one who agreed," said Craig. "Personally, I'd rather be back at the Cat playing what we want."

"Larry, listen to me man. I want to be here," Mac said as he got up and walked away from his makeup mirror toward me. "But I got no songs. Not doing any of my R&B tunes, Isley Brothers shit, Wilson Pickett, Sam and Dave . . . It's freaking me out. Them's my bread and butter so it's like I ain't really here anyway the way it's goin'."

Everybody was dead serious. This was a gut-deep issue. We were almost two weeks into our four weeks here, when we should be sky high, we were basement low.

"Well, what do you want to do?" I said, palms out.

"We've got to be us," said Les. "This feels like whoring. I'm hating music right now and that never happens." Everybody was nodding.

"You know what's going to happen if we break out …?" I said.

"You gonna try to talk us out of it? Measured response, all that crap?" said Mac.

"Yeah, if I thought I could, if I didn't agree with you. We sacrificed a lot to get here. But seems like we're none of us happy here, 'at the top of the bottom,'" a nod to Les. "So, if we cut loose maybe the hotel will love us and see that we're great entertainers and that playing back to back hot sets will only improve the show. Maybe they'll realize how good we are when we do what we do. Small chance of that, of course. But if not, well maybe we just don't belong here." I stood up and met everyone's eyes.

"Damn it, I know I wouldn't book us back here the way our show's coming off right now, contract or no. We're not the Lettermen or some soft harmony group, we can't stretch our limited repertoire to make even one decent set." I sucked in air, and whooshed it out. "So okay, let's do it. Let's put together a kick-ass new set list right now."

"Fuck yeah," Mac yelled and every one quickly echoed the sentiment. Despite the fact we were going to catch a lot of flak, everybody's spirits were high as we joked around and got dressed for the stage. I felt like we were a football team filing out onto the field as we were decked out in our favorite burgundy suits. Our set list was the best of everything we had and while there was good pacing with some great vocal tunes in the set there would be no Lettermen songs tonight. As we got near the stage we could hear the crowd going wild for the Checkmates Ltd., but that was okay. We weren't bringing knives to a gun fight anymore.

## Chances Run Out

"I would like to call the next witness forward," the defense lawyer, Robert Von, stated. "Nora Collins, please come to the stand."

Susana's eyes shut tight as she sat in the court room and heard the lawyer call her best-friend before the judge. Her heart beat rapidly against her chests walls and pumped the blood through her system at an ever increasing pace. She couldn't hear a word fall form Nora's lips, too quickly had she become entranced in the memory that was now this case.

\*\*\*

His voice low and slow lured her toward his company but continued only to sting her with malice. His words, sharp like knives, pierced her with fear. Trees blew in the cool autumn air but the wind brought no other voices along. She knew she was all alone; she was all alone to fight; and all alone to survive.

Hot breath that reeked of earlier drinks filled her nostrils. The burning liquid that he had consumed clouded his judgment and made her sick to her stomach. The stench burned her senses and, furthermore, left her to loathe his presence.

Metallic blood filled her taste buds when he bit her lip in a forceful kiss. Along with the former taste came the harsh burn of alcohol that still rested on his tongue. The bitter tastes mixed and turned her stomach. She felt bile rise in her throat just as the flavors left.

Her body pled to be absent from this scene, for her to be any where else, but rather froze in panic from his declaration. Her mind screamed to run, to yell, to do anything, but nothing was emitted from her lips. She stood there with tears that drowned her bright, emerald green eyes as her body shook. All fight removed from her will.

Thumping pain engulfed her face when she was hit. Sharp pain trapped her arms and chest as he bit her over and over again. Throbbing pain shot through her back as he pushed her against the car's dark green frame. Agony ripped through her as he brought her

65

within her car but the tormentor had only just begun.

Tearing sounds surrounded the inner walls of the car as she had unwillingly been freed of her clothes. Yells covered the ripping of the garments. However, the loudest sound had been one that couldn't be heard, it had been the silence of the most important voice, the same voice that would later speak of guilt.

\*\*\*

Robert and Nora's voices buzzed quietly in Susana's ears. She had told and heard the facts too many times to count and she couldn't stand the pain that plunged with them. Her eyes burned with stinging tears as the aftermath pushed its way through to her main fore.

\*\*\*

Shuddering on the front porch of her small home, she sat finally screaming out what she wished she had when she had been forced down.

*"Stop! Please, just stop!"*

The screams now stood directed at the constant nagging voice in her head instead of him. The guilt, the fault all landed on her shoulders. She should have taken charge and said something, maybe then it wouldn't have happened. He was intoxicated no doubt while she cried and sat sober. She should have screamed; she should have fought! Maybe someone would have heard; would have helped!

Silence had done her no good and when she had spoken up, had she been right to say what had happened? He hadn't been sane at the time it occurred and hadn't it been her duty to have stopped it? She would be taking time from his life to be lived, pressing charges would ruin the rest of the life he had ahead. How selfish could she possibly be? He had done no wrong; clearly he had been driven by liquor. Had he been sober would this have happened, surely not.

The guilt and blame ate at her like salt water ate a freshly painted boat. Before long she would be eaten altogether and sink into the pits of oblivion. Everyone around told her to keep fighting; told her he would get what he deserved… but was it wrong of her to hope he would be given freedom; be found innocent?

If only she had known all the wrongs he had committed sober maybe she wouldn't have blamed herself and let herself sink into that oblivion. Of all the sufferers, she was the one that pushed the hardest and felt the most guilt; was the one who fought to make his chances run out.

## Twelve Grapes at Midnight

On the day I turned twenty, no one wished me a happy birthday.

It was Christmas break and I was alone in northern Spain. Transatlantic calls were expensive in 1966, so I hadn't talked to my family since I'd left Indiana four months earlier to attend the University of Madrid. Three days later I would spend Christmas alone, then I planned to return to Madrid by New Year's Eve. I wanted to follow the local custom for bringing good luck in the coming year. I would go to the Puerta del Sol in the heart of the city, and pop twelve grapes—one for each stroke of the clock—into my mouth.

Spain jangled like an alarm clock, waking me from my Midwestern dream. All romantic notions—sunny skies, flouncy skirts, brave matadors—had succumbed to the realities of life in Madrid, a teeming city that sweltered in summer, then turned rainy in fall and cold in winter. I got around town by descending into the subways, where crowds, acrid odors, deafening screeches and the clattering of metal wheels overwhelmed my senses. On the streets above, few trees grew, except in parks; and the incessant traffic turned the air filthy. When I shampooed my hair in the shower, the rinse water ran black down the drain.

At first everything shocked me: Spanish girlfriends kissing each other hello on both cheeks and walking arm in arm through the crush of pedestrians; blind people selling long streamers of lottery tickets they wore pinned to their chests; Gypsy women and children sprawling on the sidewalk, begging for pesetas; men with no legs, casualties of the Civil War, perambulating by putting their fists down on the sidewalk and swinging their torso forward.

One night during my first week, after being out with friends, I came home alone, walking the last few blocks from the subway stop. The streets were deserted except for a few taxis, their headlights illuminating the uneven stone blocks of the pavement. I arrived at my building to find the door locked. I had no key. Remembering what my landlady had told me, I clapped my hands and waited. Nothing happened, so I clapped again, louder. At last, a man in a shabby uniform emerged from the darkness, jingling a gigantic ring of keys. After giving me the once-over, he selected one, let me in, then held out his hand for a few pesetas. Thus I met the *sereno,* the night watchman assigned to my block.

Generalísimo Francisco Franco had clenched the reins of government in the three decades since the Spanish Civil War. It was common to see machine-gun-toting *Guardia Civil* in green uniforms and patent leather hats patrolling streets and train stations. At hotels, guests surrendered passports to the desk clerk who registered them with the police during the night. In the Spanish version of *The Sound of Music,* censors cut the singing-nun scene for being subversive and anti-Catholic. Citizens over 30 who had survived the Civil War liked the stability that Franco represented, or perhaps they simply feared speaking out against him. But it was the Sixties; the younger generation of Spaniards wanted more freedom.

Every weekday I rode the *tranvía,* an old-fashioned streetcar with wooden seats and floors, to the Ciudad Universitaria for classes in history, literature and art. I strained to comprehend the professors' rapid-fire Spanish, wrote page after page of notes in blue spiral notebooks, and somehow managed to pass exams. Professors, who often smoked while lecturing, didn't take roll or give daily assignments. The buildings had no clocks. A man called a *bedel* knocked on the door when the hour was up and said, *"Es la hora."*

Often I'd get to campus to find mounted policemen, called *grises* from their gray uniforms, rounding up small bands of rock-hurling students. Another *huelga* meant no classes that day. If the strike took place on a Thursday, the university also closed down on Friday, which freed up long weekends for travel. My girlfriends and I took trains to Toledo and Barcelona and hitchhiked to Portugal. We went to Granada and Malaga, then boarded a boat for Morocco, just to say we'd been to Africa.

One weekend, the history professor took a group of students to Segovia and Salamanca. I went because I'd fallen in love with an American boy in the class. I knew Rich had a girlfriend back home in Wisconsin, but I was the one sitting next to him in class and on the *tranvía.* He kissed me for the first time in Salamanca as we stood on the banks of the Río Tormes, the lights of the city reflecting in the black water, a bright moon overhead illuminating the ancient stone bridge.

Rich was part of the reason my roommate, Joanna, and I didn't get along. I suspected she liked him too. And I was jealous—I envied her fluent Spanish and her ease in social situations. Two weeks after the trip to Salamanca, Rich invited me to an Arthur Rubenstein concert at the Teatro Nacional. I became ill at the last minute. As I had no way to get in touch with him, I asked Joanna to take my place. Sitting on the cold linoleum, vomiting into the toilet, I felt sad and angry, yet noble that I'd given her my ticket. The nausea had passed by the time Joanna came home, and when she told me about the concert, the seed of a guarded friendship began to grow.

Despite our differences, Joanna and I scoured the neighborhood together in search of snacks. We headed to the *pastelería* for cream-filled pastries or to the potato chip factory down the street. It had a sales office, only slightly wider than its doorway. A dour woman with dyed red hair sat behind the glass counter which was filled with potato chips. She'd funnel some into a paper cone and tell us the price. She never smiled or acknowledged us even after several months. Thinking back, I know she must have had a name and a history, maybe several doting grandchildren. Perhaps in her younger years she'd danced Flamenco or acted in the *zarzuela*, but to me she was simply a neighborhood fixture who existed solely to sell me potato chips.

At Christmas break, my friends went skiing in the Alps, but I was too broke to join them. I traveled alone to spend my twentieth birthday and Christmas in Northern Spain. Rain and loneliness made for a depressing holiday, but the week I spent exploring Burgos, San Sebastian, Santander and Santiago de Compostela gave me time to reflect. I realized that everything I was and everything I believed was an accident of birth. If I'd been born in Spain, my patriotic feelings would be for Spain. If I'd been born into a Catholic family I would say the rosary. If I'd been born into poverty, I might sell lottery tickets in the subway. On the train back to Madrid I felt the surge of a new strength. I controlled my own future. I didn't have to play out a role dictated by church or parents or convention.

By the time the warm breezes of spring arrived, I felt like a *madrileña*. I no longer mentally converted pesetas into dollars. I knew that if the thermometer topped 30 degrees, it was too hot; if my weight rose above 60 kilos, I needed to cut back on *pasteles*. I ignored the men who said suggestive things to me on the streets, or if they tried to grab me, could cut them down in Spanish. I craved the taste of squid sandwiches and *boquerones*, tiny deep-fried fish I gobbled—bones and all. When I ordered *vino tinto y una ración de queso manchego*, waiters thought I was Spanish. I saw nothing unusual in watching six bulls get stabbed and dragged from the ring on a Sunday afternoon. It seemed commonplace now, when coming home late, to clap for the *sereno*.

In June, students dispersed to travel around Europe and then go back to the States. Joanna and I remained close after we returned home, but my relationship with Rich, sustained for a while with post-cards and letters, eventually faded away.

Not long ago I came across three blue spiral notebooks in the attic. A chill came over me when I opened them. The pages were covered with handwriting I recognized as my own, yet it might as well have been written by a stranger as I could no longer comprehend all of it. But even though I've forgotten much of the Spanish language, I remember what it was like to live in Spain. In fact, there is an eternal map of Spain in the back of my mind with vivid memories pinned to it, memories triggered by a whiff of olive oil, a taste of saffron or the strumming of a flamenco guitar. Spain is where my character took shape. I learned what it felt like to be a foreigner. I lost my fear of being alone.

Now, I'm approaching the age the potato chip lady was then. The kids in my neighborhood probably see me as the bicycle lady or the lady-with-a-camera. They don't know I hitchhiked around Europe or that I spent my twentieth birthday and Christmas alone. Or that on New Year's Eve I straddled the back of a motorcycle, prowling the streets of Madrid and ending up at the Puerta del Sol at midnight.

It's not easy downing a dozen grapes in the time it takes a clock to clang twelve times. But I joined thousands of other *madrileños* that night to give it a try. Good fortune followed; the sweet, lucky juice burst from the grapes, dripped off my chin and drizzled through the rest of my life.

71

MARIE GRIFFITHS

# Raiders in the Night

Amid-June night and jasmine masks freeway exhaust fumes
and strip mall scents hanging over north Fontana, neighborhoods
of ticky-tacky homes on tiny plots, cinder-blocked against Santa Ana
harassment. In this concrete-ordered world, a garden hewn from
stony ground and a few young trees struggle to flourish, save one.
Burdened by bounty, branches bent like a gaudy Christmas tree,
drooping, weary of its peachy orbs, it is a true prize husbanded
by an insomniac gardener. She has for days fretted, carefully
balancing danger of bough breakage against perfection of ripeness.
Now aroused by rustling outside her open window and the distinctive
crunch of sharp teeth meeting fruit stone, she ventures from bedroom
safety into vernal night. Ensconced in the middle of the little peach tree,
two white-faced, long-snouted, natty-furred, rat-tailed possums sit
frozen by flashlight beams. Marsupial intruders ignore the gardener's
aggressive stance and threats just as they disregard concrete boundaries.
Flinching just once when a stone hits home, they vacate their bower
only when hosed, nozzle on jet. In the morn, she ruthlessly strips the tree
bare of its near-succulent harvest. Sun and Sky witness her vow, *No nectar
will there be this year for me, and, possums, none will there be for thee!*

# Spirit Wave

Looming out of blackness,
ever nearer, a titan surges.
Shadow woman
takes my hand. Our urge

stronger than tsunami,
we swim up its face,
over white-topped crest,
or must die the sailor's death.

Once innocents, we were
rocked in the wine-dark cradle,
and floated without fear
of fathoms.

Tides marked the passage
of our days and of our nights,
while we drifted light
as balsa wood atop the deep.

At last, caught in the current
of Ocean's ambiguity,
open-eyed but blind to knowing
sparkling surface

from sandy bottom, we are
pummeled and surf-churned,
our breath bubbles nearly gone,
our lives become a shipwreck.

Tonight we dream again –
flailing, thrashing, hurling
ourselves up the water wall,
migrating towards our destiny.

# Blue Envy

Molten blob born of sand
and Vulcan's fire, glowing
red on the tip of a rod,
your maker's breath blowing
you into transparent form,
shaping your neck, fluted,
your round body, smooth,
comely, with just enough heft
to fill a woman's cupped hand –
too demure to hold more than
an aromatic nosegay of violets –
you cooled to a rich blue

not quite royal or sapphire,
more like the deep indigo sea
that sloshes against shallow turquoise
on the far side of Polynesian atolls,
the very shade of breast feathers
on peacocks guarding the gates of paradise
and of irises in all-seeing eyes
winking from their tail feathers,
iridescent in shafts of light – yet –

non-sentient artifact of antiquity,
you can have no memory
of the first careful caress of her hands,
or of slim fingers pinging your rim
just to hear you sing, no impression
of the many hands that once marveled
at your beauty, all long since become
spindly white bones folded in repose.

Neither are *you* immortal.
One day your mystique will shatter –
in an instant, nothing, but cobalt shards
scattered across a hard cold floor.

# Mississippi Memory

We was boys outta breath
a-racin' to Catfish Pond.

We flop on the damp bank, close
and so still I hear every croak, quack
and splash. I can hear a cottonmouth
wriggle through the rushes.

I study the whiteness where your
shirt open, so white it dazzle the sun.
I mess up your fine pale hair.
You grab my hand away from there,
pull it tight to your belly.

I lean over you near as red
dragonflies skim the water.
You say I stink like pond mud.
I don't pay no never mind
and just laugh. My strong pink tongue
flick over closed eyes, count freckles,
lick sweat from off your brow.

Then, like a bass breakin' the surface,
you jump straight up, spillin' me off.
You let out a whoop loud 'nough to
startle the sparrows still.
I let out a whoop of my own.

You shrug off your shirt,
dance outta your shorts and wade in.
You tell me, "Randy, get on in here!"
You say a big ole' catfish be swimin'
'tween your legs, touchin' you

with his whiskers.
But I stay on shore, stiff
as the brown-tipped bull rushes.

We was boys together and you
was my onliest Lyle.

# January in Vermont

In the milky distance
a stand of conifers,
sole remnants
of summer's hue,
draped anew
in soft folds of ermine,
lapse into monochromatic scape.

A pair of crows perched
on the wrought iron bough
of a sugar maple
unsettle a small clump of snow
by their sudden departure,
leaving the branch twice barren,
caws shattering frozen,
glass-fragile quietude.

Flaxen-pale light shed
by the anemic sun glints
off steely ax but cannot warm
the woodsman whose Wellingtons
crunch across blasted fields, nor
the bones of small burrowed varmints
blindly trusting a covenant:

that under winter's thick down
a dormant mystery gestates.

# "La Dame" sans Merci

Blustery whore on a mission,
she bangs through each street and yard
in Fontana and messes
with every kind of trash.

After a dalliance, the bitch
uses tumble weeds as flinty
fingernails, scratching the paint
of shiny new sedans.

Dominatrix on a binger,
she whips palm fronds into frenzy,
snaps saplings and uproots stately
eucalypti.

Voracious, she strips roses bare,
humps fences flat with lusty thrusts
and scours the ground, belching
clouds of fine sand.

Squinting against her gritty gusts,
dry as mummies we cry,
*Lotion and lip balm!* – quite undone
by La Dame's velocity.

**KELLY SMITH**

## The Violinist and the Purple Tiger

The violinist played beautiful music but only when she danced. She would play and dance from morning until night. Her violin was purple, which pleased her so. A tiger slipped quietly out of the jungle and into the clearing. It wanted to see what was making that beautiful noise. The violinist saw the tiger and was not afraid. She was intrigued by his color. For you see, the tiger was purple, which pleased her so.

The violinist had a bucket full of papayas by her side, for she had heard tigers like papayas, especially purple tigers. The tiger gave a low growl as it stared curiously at the violinist. It lay down beside her and listened to the beautiful music. The violinist continued playing her violin and she danced until the sun set in the western sky. She reached into a bucket and brought out a papaya and gave it to the purple tiger. For you see, tigers like papayas, especially purple tigers.

Thus begins the friendship between a violinist with a purple violin and a purple tiger. The tiger enjoyed the music so much that it let the violinist dance on his back while she played her beautiful music. The violinist could hear the tiger chuffing, which pleased her so. For you see, since tigers roar they cannot purr. Chuffing is the tiger's way of showing the violinist he likes her and they are friends, which pleased her so.

Every evening the violinist laid down her purple violin. She would feed the tiger a bucket full of fresh, ripe papayas, of course. Nothing more, nothing less, for you see, papayas are a purple tiger's favorite fruit.

## Miles from the Past

It's just as mother warned—
you'd never even know the way
Stop trying to rebuild the past
I will tell you what it's become

The pavement leads away from town
past shredding billboards, the droning
hum of silence along a row of tattered
Eucalyptus trees and stubble grass

The town's back is pressed flat
against the rolling hills, lapped
by rusting tracks and broken ties
waiting for trains that never come

Brick-brown buildings ramble down
one side of Front Street, then fade
into ghost weeds and yester berries
scraggling along old Highway 66

Mother road maunders over the heartland
searching for some final place of rest
to watch her blacktop puzzle and crack
in the crematory afternoon

# How Will I Finally Learn?

I could read it in the paper one day too late
after I might have said *goodbye*
and *you must have known I loved you*
*with all the wisdom of a life that never was.*

A black sedan would drive to my street
someone who knew—a friend perhaps—
would knock at my front door
tell me something has gone wrong.

The world has tilted one last degree
and you are gone as if you'd never
looked at me, dark eyes full
of promises we never had the chance to keep.

Will he paraphrase my tears
understand I knew you better than those
who walked beside you through the years?
Will he realize, who cannot know, that my world is overgrown

with the garden we never planted
the foundation we never laid
as he stumbles upon me, on my knees, still
wishing the colors of our once upon world?

# in Lusty-
## spring

I caught my garden growing wild

The zucchini stretched    an inch   or two

today in the morning sun

bragging

its manly

length


and not to be outdone

the yellow squash
                bent its head

around the planter's edge

      Its golden blossoms winked in their fun,

                flinging care
                    to the Santa Anas
and changed from cups to saucers


I caught the beans
           vibrating free

from their vertical restraints

while tomatoes blushed in lofty grandstands

bashful beside the white-washed shed

# Chocolate Mint Leaves

Soft ears, long-veined purple ribs,
serrated edges on flexible spines—
someone is playing a trick on me.

I rub the deep green leaves,
ease out summer delight
from my heart's treasury:

Those days before we conditioned air
on sweltering August nights,
sprinklers on the neighbor's lawn till ten,

Polka-dots of lightning bugs in jars,
illuminating our way back home
till we set them free on our front stoop.

I breathe in great white bowls,
slice a pint in four cold slabs,
one for each of us around the kitchen table,

Chocolate mint ice cream, chopped and stirred
to soft serve under the whirring kitchen fan,
our one cool spot on earth.

Childhood's nightly renascence.

# Halfway: A Marital Dialogue

I'm going to the top this time.

*Stay where you are, you old coot; you'll fall.*

Last time, I didn't break a thing.

*You were nineteen.*

What could break?

*Plenty. That's far enough.*

It was your words
scared me off the second limb.

*You're high enough to break a limb or two.*

I've got no breakables—no eggs in my pocket,
no heart on my sleeve,no dreams in my head.

*Your head is as thick as that trunk and you're twice as barky; get down.*

Good thing my head *is* thick, keeps me alive
Nothing breakable there.

*Nothing but our home.*

Don't kid yourself, girlie—empty ain't no home.

*Give me half a whisper
and we'll nest again.*

Whisper? Whisp is all that's left, ball of fluff,
stuff trussed up in a bow only you could tie
around our bygone dang-
ling clutter.

*Should have tied you down,*
*trussed those silly wings long ago.*

I want to fly.

*Get down. That is far enough.*

Halfway     is     never     far     enough.

# Morfar's porch

He didn't care much for perfection
no character, he'd say.
His porch was full of messy things:
Morning glories escaping their trellises,
screen door made of creaky hinges
and the slam-bump-bump of goodbye,
flaked white swing where we shared books,
the sweet weight of wisdom in our hands,
most afternoons, lemonade or licorice tea, and once,
the ruddy surprise of my first pomegranate,
rough and weathered as his Pennsylvania rail yard hands.

*A special treat, lilla vän,* he said,
*all the way from the sun in California.*
But it didn't look like treat, more
like sin—red, blotchy, too ugly
to be very good—lumpy and leaden as it lay
in my tiny hand, crumbling crown-full
of what looked like critters from his musty cellar.
*Wait.* He slipped his retirement knife
out of the overalls pocket,
split the leather fruit, and oh!
Some things are better than perfection.

# Last Train from Renovo, PA

Steam whistle wails through the hills,
wrapping her deeper in darkness
farther and farther from home.

In the distance, a farmhouse,
circle of light from one room,
beacon of warmth in the moonless sweep
of November sky.

Wheels click-clack, rock, and groan,
Cradling with somnolent gloom,
one woman in black, alone.

# Terminal Chicago

No one seemed to see the two of us against the wall
waiting for our separate planes at Midway in Chicago
the last time we were together. I remember
watching those who passed that night
envying the beauty of the everyday—
shared spaces, the world without partings
small gestures of their indifferences. I pressed
against your  chest and thighs without asking
because they were our final moments. No one
cared how close we stood, how we ignored
the phones that held those other lives we knew
waiting on both sides of a gleaming comet's ride.
I shivered at the entrance gate. You offered
your sweatshirt, blue and green; I took it
not for warmth but for a scent of us
along the sleeves. I clung to it and asked
*Should I send it somewhere when I arrive*? You said
*Keep it* because you knew I'd need it later.

We didn't speak much after that. At the gate,
we kissed our last message, *ILY Goodbye*.
I handed you the journal we had kept
then pulled my bag
along the aching tunnel to the door, never
looking back. I walked with eyes ahead
exhausted, so quiet I could hear your wish
to call me back, your willing me to turn.
I put the sweatshirt on and settled in my seat
looking out at blackness in the tiny window
above the wing. Then I thought I saw your coat
hands pressed against the terminal panes, felt certain
that you loved me. After that, I sipped my tea
and I was traveling alone, living on the warmth
the scent of you and me in blue and green.

# Coco

"Hey, Pete, have you seen my cat?" my neighbor Margo asks as I hose down the driveway.

"Because Fluffy didn't come home last night."

"No," I lie. Coco cornered and killed Fluffy yesterday. I buried the calico under the maple in our backyard late last night. Coco. A demon rat terrier straight from hell.

The damn dog only weighs ten pounds. He's brown and white with short wiry hair and maybe eight inches at the shoulder, but he can jump like a flea, with a vertical leap of (I measured it) five-plus feet. Last week he high-jumped into my recently restored classic boat and chewed his way through the shiny new upholstery. The ingestion of same gave him diarrhea, which he managed to unload all over the area rug. Insult to injury, he yakked up gooey chunks of foam and vinyl on the couch.

Although Julia and Emily object, Coco has a date with the pound. My wife and daughter refuse to accept the reality that there is nothing about Coco worth loving. The neighbor's cat is the final nail in Coco's coffin. The demon dog has to go. I hope, without a single flinch, that he'll get a lethal injection.

At the animal shelter, Coco, slippery devil, escapes when I open the car door. He careens, yapping madly, around the parking lot like a barrel racer. I swear I hear him chortle as he shoots between my legs and avoids the grabbing hands of a hooting teenager who jumps off a skateboard to assist in the capture.

The commotion draws the attention of an employee. An old geezer with silver stubble and a gold hoop in one ear exits the building. The geezer smirks, as if he sees this every day.

He pulls a long leash from his back pocket, shakes it out and fashions a slip knot. Transformed into Cowboy Bob, the old man swirls the coil over his head like a calf roper. He waits, waits, throws.

The loop floats on angel wings across the blacktop and drops precisely over Coco's head. Cowboy Bob snugs the line and reels him in. Coco, entirely uncool with the whole operation, erupts like a hooked swordfish. He shimmies and twists, but his captor is relent-less.

Coco continues to thrash at the end of the leash, unheeded by the man who steadily pulls him closer. Spitting a thin stream of brown saliva, he eyes me as if I'm something he just stepped in. Like tobac-co juice.

"This your dog?"

I nod.

"You dropping him?"

Another nod.

"Come inside then. Fill out a form." He turns for the door. Coco resists, now bringing to mind a brick tied to a piece of rope.

A car pulls into the parking area. A woman and a young boy exit a newer model pale blue Buick. She's in her forties with platinum curls and a tight tee that says *Give Peace a Chance* tucked into skin-ny jeans over three-inch wedges. The boy is maybe ten. A long pelt of shiny mahogany hair hangs in eyes that never leave the tips of his Vans. His jeans ride low on narrow hips. She looks from Cowboy Bob to Coco, to me. "Are you getting rid of that dog?"

Again I nod. Words don't seem necessary.

"He's just the cutest thing," she exhales. I get an impression of breathless delight on a gust of peppermint scented breath. She hugs her truculent son to her side. "Isn't he just what we were looking for, Tony?"

Tony gives Coco, who's impersonating a thrown retread, a disinterested glance. "No. He looks dead."

"You trained him didn't you?" Tony's mom smiles at me. "He can do other tricks I bet. Fetch, shake hands, that sort of thing?"

I shrug.

A corner of Bob's mouth ticks up.

Scooping Coco up, I put him in her arms. "His name is Coco. You'll love him." I run to my car, jump in and peel out before anyone can ask my name.

# JANIS YOUNG

## I Could Have Married

I could have married a stubby little man, irregular featured and forgettable, whose hands and feet were even smaller than my own. Quick to smile and compliment, he was unable to hide flashes of desire when he looked at me, but I pretended not to notice.

It was his kindness toward me that kept me off balance, a weakness that made me stay when I should have gone. His kindness was a numbing, murderous charity, a novelty that shut down my intellect and paralyzed the mechanics of thought. I only felt. I don't know what. And that was his trick, the trick that transformed me and began changing me into someone else.

Lying under a rumpled sheet, after we had finally been together, I saw him naked and vulnerable. I looked at the blue-veined, hairless backs of his knees, and the scar on his back. How does someone get a scar like that? He was disgusting. I was a fool. He wasn't right for me at all, and he was crippling me with kind words and affectionate gestures.

To save myself I fled back to my world, back to intelligent assessments and critical evaluations, back to a world peopled with the right men. He may have cried. I really don't know because I just don't remember.

And now, years later, shipwrecked and shattered by the right men, I wonder what I ran from? If I had given in to him and had let him use the saw of tenderness to dismember me limb by limb, and if I had then let him cobble me back together, piece by piece, an entirely new person, what creature could I have become? Who would I be now? What did I run from? What have I done?

93

# The Dress

She hung her brown, calico dress carefully in the dark corner, on the wooden hook worn smooth by the touch of many hands. The style was simple enough. The dress had a large V shaped yoke both front and back, which fell down past her shoulders. There full sleeves began in tiny, painstaking gathers and draped the length of her arms, ending at her wrists. The bodice and skirt of the dress were one piece and were attached to the bottom edge of the yoke, creating a graceful fullness. The volume of the skirt could be easily cinched in with a blue sash for her wedding, but it could also be left unbelted later to accommodate a swollen body, due to the good news of a coming baby.

She had painstakingly made it, laboring many hours with needle and thread, shaping and fitting the yard goods her mother had carefully kept for her since she was a little girl. Once she pricked her finger, a vividly remembered sting. A drop of blood still stained the left sleeve, down near the hem. She knew exactly where the small stain was located and occasionally looked at it thoughtfully. It was just as much a part of the dress as the soft feel of the fabric, its dull sheen, and the faint scent of camphor.

She had worked on the dress at odd moments. Sometimes, when she was between chores, she would stitch and inch or two more of a seam. Other times, at night by candle light, she rhythmically worked the strong thread in and out, to create tiny, perfect stitches. An old frontier saying declared that a woman could be wed, bred, and dead in the same dress. No doubt she would wear the dress on her wedding day, with orange blossoms in her hair, if there were any orange blossoms to be had. Later, if a baby came, the dress would become a comfortable friend, easing her through the anticipation of that time. It was clearly understood by the girl that the dress would probably become her shroud as well, the garment used to clothe her in a cold grave beneath the grassy, green prairie sod.

But that was alright with her. It was her dress, and it would be hers until the end, and she knew even beyond that. It was hers and hers alone, a labor of her own hands, the work of her youth as she waited for her life to begin.

# Kosmos, Palms

INLANDIA CREATIVE WRITING WORKSHOP - PALM SPRINGS
LED BY MAUREEN ALSOP

CONTRIBUTORS

Cynthia Anderson
Jaqueline Mantz Rodriguez
Tami Sigurdson
Gillian Spedding

## Ordinary Doves

The world is full
of ordinary doves
who arrive like
something they're not—

Puffed up in the cold
to twice their size
and landing in a swirl
of feathers.

They sit perfectly still,
immovable—for once,
no fussing or fighting,
no cooing calls.

That one, on a rocky outcrop,
tries to imitate a hawk—
the hunch, the chiseled profile,
the turn of the head.

As the sun lifts higher,
he preens and fidgets,
the heat seeping into
his witless brain.

A vague hunger stirs.
There was something
he meant to do—
but what?

An ordinary day
with its petty battles
is already unfolding.

It's time to descend
from the heights
and engage.

## JACQUELINE MANTZ RODRIGUEZ

# Daddy Sings Bacon

As I cook macadamia nut pancakes, applewood bacon and eggs over medium I listen to Johnny Cash, one of my daddy's favorites. The taste of my breakfast is sweet as I put Knott's boysenberry syrup on my pancakes. When I crunch a piece of bacon and close my eyes in ecstasy my *big talking* daddy is at the stove. Grease is everywhere, he does not use lids, my daddy, when cooking. There is grease on his white stained t-shirt, grease in the pan and grease on the paper towel hiding underneath that bacon, that bacon that winks to me in the Sunday morning. My daddy, John, can *walk that line* between unhygienic and home cooking. None of us girls ever got food poisoning even though the pans were never thoroughly cleaned by my mom and my dad smoked as he cooked.

"Girls, breakfast is ready. Come eat now..."

My dad was pretty laid back except when it came to food. He wanted us to eat while it was hot. We would run in in our pajamas and sit at our glass table. My mom would come in and we would all eat as a family. My parents seemed to have more problems than answers. Yet, I see now at forty that we were a family and for that I am so grateful.

*Just five people, that's all we were, trying to make a family out of chaos, we'd get together at that family table eating loud, eating did help all our troubled souls. We were a circle,* I see now a circle where daddy cooked, mom ate and us girls rejoiced and prayed we could come together like this for more than food, for fun and be at peace.

Today, I sit with my own family, My puppy Elizabeth, Lizzy as I call her, sits in my lap and steals bacon from me just like I did with my dad. I do know she is just a dog but she is a sort of child. My Joe eats his pancakes and bacon separately from the eggs. I ask him if the food is good.

"I bought the bacon from the butcher at Stater Brothers. Is it worth $4.99 a pound.?

Joe nods and gets up to get more bacon so I am satisfied.

Lizzy will eat as much bacon as I give her. I understand now why my daddy loved to cook for us. *By and By* I have come to understand now why the loss of family time at the table in modern times is such a travesty.

*One of these days, it won't be long I am going to rejoin my daddy at that table...*

\*\*\*

*Note: Lines influenced by Johnny Cash are italicized.*

*Songs quoted: Ring of Fire, Going to Jackson, Walk the Line, and Daddy Sang Base*

# Ode to Five Guys

Very rarely, there comes along something new,
Not something borrowed or blue,
but something precious.
For many of us,
Life is a series of mediocre experiences
Broken bottles of love, pseudo pink slime pattties—
For some of us, we occasionally meet—pieces
Of experience, that put a ring on our finger
Those experiences that linger
Forever and ever.

Such was it was with Five Guys,

Tablecloth red and white checkered building bold against a sunrise

Fresh fried potatoes and burgers so delicious—In and Out seems
Like a wood pecker pecking on a plastic tree, you feel me.

Eat this, a cheeseburger with lettuce, tomato, pickles and raw onion
Wait I haven't even begun
Then I can add mayo, ketchup and even jalapeños.
That's all I do folks but if you wanna have some more fun,
There's mushrooms, A1, BBQ sauce, relish and green peppers,
I could go on and on and on forever.
Made fresh to order and while you wait even eat peanuts in the
shell,
This is fast food heaven not McDonald's hell.

Once upon a French fry, this is no ordinary potato
Fresh cut regular or even Cajun, man oh man
hot upon the roof of the mouth—so,
Delicious God would say God Damm!

So, let your mouth linger and lick those fingers as life—
is something new something to prove that there is a God,
Still alive and well in the world, preaching peace and love without strife.
Jesus, would bless these fries and give them to his apostles, the
masses, the poor, down trodden—like the fish—fries for life.
French fries pouring out of brown paper bags for evermore...

Very rarely comes along something new,
A transcendent experience, so precious,
This memory true,
The words I shall say as I do not go gentle,
Eros, I want some fries, a burger from five guys...

# Stories

I'm writing a fictional story right now based on my brother's death. As I question my mom on the particulars she tells me she hates to speak about tragedy.

"I don't like to talk about it. I hate to put tragedy on people. I only talk about what happened with David with close friends," she says.

If you know my mother then you would understand that this is unusual. There are typically no conversations off limits with my mother. She tells a stranger of her bladder issues or talks about her sex life with her daughters without being asked.

So, why is it so hard for people to talk about our dark times? My mother had never told me the full story of my brother David's death. He died a few years before I was born. All I ever saw was his grave. I had no idea he was good at puzzles and could fix mechanical things. I did not know that David used to sleep in the same bed as my mom and cuddled close to her like a puppy during the cold rainy nights in Portland, Oregon. How could I know that my mom left everything she had,; all her family, friends and belongings behind, for her son who was five years old, deaf, and in need of help.

After hearing the entire tale, which I will not retell, I write my own story. In it she is a heroic tragic figure who yearns to one day tell her son the stories she remembers her mother telling her before she died. You see, my grandmother died when my mom was fourteen. Maybe that is why she doesn't tell her stories to her daughters or maybe we just need to ask.

# If Only

*If Onlys* are like hard sticky candies stuck between one's teeth, they take so long to dissolve. I doubt this one ever will.

My firstborn Eloy is all thin face, thinking eyes and caramelized butterscotch skin, all soft wispy curls. He watches me all the time with his large cup of coffee eyes. When Eloy turns two I learn something is wrong. Not regular wrong but I am going to leave everything I know behind wrong.

A nurse comes by to check on Eloy and says, "Something is wrong with this child." His hands are wrong. I still don't know what she meant by this as she looked at his palms and shook her head. The next morning I take Eloy to the William Tracy clinic in Los Angeles. All he can hear is vibrations. I hold him and just cry. Eloy's dad, a good for nothing fool, says to me when I tell him the news, "Let's take him to a home and get this over with, he's damaged goods." I left soon after as Eloy may be damaged but he is my son. The first thing I try is the local school for the deaf. Riverside's School for the Deaf does not take him. They are full and he is too young. I wait, waiting drives me crazy. Eloy is not communicating and he hides from me many days. I fear something will happen to him when I am at work. After waiting and working for two years with my brother, I decide to go to Portland, Oregon. At five years old, Eloy is a waif of a wind whirl with a muted voice but his eyes speak desperate frustration; we must go.

I take the bus to Portland, Oregon with two hundred dollars in my pocket and one suitcase. It is cold and my Orange County California sweater is not warm enough. I tuck the covers around Eloy and try to sleep on the bus. My appointment at the Oregon school for the deaf is the next day. I find us a one-bedroom house in Portland, Oregon on 62$^{nd}$ street for fifty dollars a month so I must find a job, quick. It rains and I walk the wet rainy streets to my job at a laundry after I walk Eloy to school. I fold clothes and I make a dollar fifty an hour. It bores me but it is enough to live on, for now. During the day Eloy goes to school. At night, he runs away from me laughing silently. I walk into my room one night and he is tearing up my rent money. Spanking him makes me feel awful and luckily he can't hear my yells. He shies away from me when he sees my angry face but we sleep together in the same bed.

One Saturday night Lorna my neighbor watches my son so I can go out to the bar on the corner. I walk into Elsie's by myself. There are two pool tables and darts. It is a typical redneck bar. There are round scarred wood tables and a long counter. Bingo is about to start. The prize is not money but food. I wear a blue mini-dress. I have flats on and I show off my legs with net stockings. I look around and I see couples all around decorating the tables with their tongues in and out of each other. I sit at the bar and nurse my fifteen-cent beer. A man comes up and sits by me. He is of average height and weight with a pale nice face and blue green eyes. He has on a blue country western shirt and jeans. I like him even though he is smoking a cigarette.

"Are you from Montana? I'm from Montana. You look Indian," he says. "My name is William."

"I'm not from Montana, I'm a Mexican from California, my name is Maria but I go by Marie," I reply. We continue talking and playing Bingo and William wins a chicken in a can.

"If you come over I'll make you this chicken for dinner," William offers as he pays for my beers and walks me home.

"Oh, you can cook, "I ask.

"I love to cook. I make good mashed potatoes too," William says.

When I go home I tell Eloy about William. He may not be able to hear but I know he understands and for the first time in a long time I think maybe all will be ok.

William picks me up at my front door. He has a blue Ford truck. William tells me all about himself. He is thirty-five and drives a freight truck for a living. His mom and dad still live in Montana. His mom is sick and he needs to go home soon to see her. William is open and honest. He listens as I tell him about my son. He nods and drives as I tell William my son is deaf and we are here for him to go to school.

"I like kids. Doesn't matter if they can't hear. They can feel love. I love hugs. William squeezes my hand. I look away. My mom died when I was ten so I find it hard to remember hugs. All I remem-

105

ber are her stories she told to me when I was a little girl and they are of no use. I squeeze his hand back. We arrive at his home. He has a little house like me. I go inside and I can tell he had cleaned up the place. The house is devoid of decoration. All he has is a card table in the kitchen with two chairs, an old checked couch and two TVs sitting one on top of the other.

He sits me down, gives me a soda pop and I watch him finish cooking. It smells good. A man has never cooked for me. I like the way he sets the chicken down in the middle of the table by the mashed potatoes, bread and margarine.

"Hope you like it,"William says, "It's nothing fancy but I don't starve. I hate eating out. This is what a home is for to sleep and eat." As we finish dinner William, now Will to me pours me a Coors and we talk amid the low din of his television set. The top set gives out the sound and the bottom set the picture, Will does not like to throw stuff away I see. I like him even more and we find our way to his bedroom.

I leave a few hours later. I have to get home to Eloy. Will says he will come by tonight to meet him and he does. Eloy looks at him and smiles as Will bends down to hug him. We date three times a week sometimes with Eloy and sometimes without if I can find a babysitter. It is three months to the day when I realize my savings is gone and I may not be able to make my rent.

"William, I don't know how to say this but Eloy and I need help. You seem like a nice man. Are you willing to take on a woman with a deaf kid?" I ask.

"Maria, I was going to ask if you and Eloy wanted to come live with me. I don't have much but what I have is yours and Eloy's from now on. I already loved him but now I love him more if that is possible. I push down the worry about his drinking. It will be ok. William is a hard worker and he, Eloy and I can make it.

William pays the bills now and I help out with groceries and the utilities. Now I can buy Eloy toys and picture books instead of just clothes. William spoils Eloy with sweets and gets lots of hugs. I watch them as they watch T.V., William drinks from a tall can of Coors and lets Eloy taste it. Eloy wrinkles his nose and spits it out. We all laugh.

Months go by and we settle into a routine. William teaches me how to play Rummy. Eloy tries to play too but he is slow in thinking and the game is hard to explain without words. William is loud and pantomimes to Eloy when he throws down the card he needs which is most of the time. William goes out some nights to the bars and I get angry.

One Friday night William is still not home. It is 6 pm and he was off at four so I know exactly where he is, at Elsie's. I feel out of control in my anger. Eloy is playing with his new toy truck in the room. I can't take it so I grab his hand and walk next door.

I knock on Lorna's door quick and fast my heart beating as I want to scream.

"Lorna, are you home?" I knock but she does not answer. Later she will tell me with tears in her voice that if only she had not been sleeping, things might have been different. I was only going to be a few minutes. I walk with David down the frigid gray streets. David pulls at my hand and looks me in the face his eyes round and dark. I look ahead angry at Will for not coming home. I rehearse what I will say.

David breaks away from me as he has done many times before. He runs and I run after him. I run, he runs into the street and a screech of breaks blocks my vision. There is a car in the middle of the street and a body on the ground. My Eloy lies in the middle of the street, twisted up like a paper straw, he is gone. I scream and my hope dies right there and passes into the afterlife with my son.

Now I sing them to my twins as they lie together in the crib. Ophelia and Jennifer are so much alike but I can tell them apart even by their smell. Ophelia is rounder and heavier. She smells sweet and heavy like a jug of milk on the doorstep. I jiggle her on my lap to make her giggle and her dimpled cheeks make me smile. Jennifer is light like a bird and smells like earth and snow. I hate Montana and I hate the cold. It reminds me of death. Death of Eloy my son. I can't think of that. I can't. I hug Ophelia too me and walk to keep the Cold thoughts away. They don't entirely leave me.

# TAMI SIGURDSON

## Despair

Morning's but begun
and the tears stream down my face
I lick my lips and swallow
the salt, a familiar taste.

The pain has broken through today
and sorrow overflows
I grapple for my glasses
and some Kleenex to wipe my nose.

I'm perspiring already
yet I've just bathed today
one of at least three times I'll try
and scrub the disease away.

The weariness is unfathomable,
how fatigue embeds my bones.
With all the love from family and friends,
I still feel completely alone.

I fumble my way to the medicine chest
to find something to take it all away
the pain that's invaded my body
and the grief I am carrying today.

I choose a clonazepam and a Tylenol #3
hoping this cocktail will provide relief
yet knowing I won't be
pain free.

For the term "chronic" is what they use
and they use it a lot,
yet I refuse to believe it applies to
the ... lasting ... symptoms that I've got.

I double over sobbing,
gasp ...
then stop to catch my breath.
It feels like a loss to me
as if I am grieving a death.

And I guess this really is a loss
for a part of me is gone
that has become more apparent
as the illness lingers on.

I've come to a fork in the road
an unexpected turn,
yet a path I was meant to travel
and lessons I need to learn.

The landscape before me lay barren
Life's treasures are littered everywhere
My heart is laden with hopelessness
This must be the place called Despair.

# Passages

The smoke trees shed indigo confetti for a Quinceañera proud with
three-hundred festive guests delighting amongst a field of palms
and Palo Verde.

A gentle elbow caress, a magnetic gaze and the memory returns,
a sultry night in the desert many years ago in this very field,

when he was swallowed up by her majestic beauty
with undulating mounds that hold delicious caverns
amid a bed of astonishing brilliant wildflowers
under a never-ending sky.

# The Landing

The pilot had told us to prepare for a hard landing. I see the roof of the airport and people looking. Maybe Joe is there. I try to wave but the crew tells us to keep our heads down. I smell smoke and burning rubber, must be a burst tire, it's ok at least we're down. Now I hear fire trucks, just a precaution. People clamber, those trucks spray foam, mind my hair! I gotta get out of here, Joe will be waiting. Where is he? Oh I get it we're far from the terminal, I guess I'll have to walk I don't see any shuttle buses, just those damn fire trucks. Where are my shoes? Shit! Where's my purse? Great now I'm going to have to call the airline. Damn no cell phone! I hope it doesn't take forever to get my stuff back. Why are the paramedics here? Oh I guess there have been some bumps and bruises, it's hard to see through this smoke. Oh my God! this girl looks really bad, quick guys over here. Hang on, those are my shoes, and why is she wearing my wedding ring?

# The Door

the door to sanity thuds shut
amid screams of yellow
and cries of burnt umber
soon *the crazy* will appear
disguised as a blank canvas
waiting for my mind to unravel

# The Crazy

the crazy comes in flashes of light
on canvas splashed with red

the crazy comes in letters
made into words
made into stories
made into poems
made into ramblings
on life
on love
on craziness

that's how it works

# Strewn

My Life Strewn
in pockets of long unworn jackets
and dusty corners of old purses.
Tickets from a concert before Jagger's face
turned gnarly wood and peace signs were in the first time.

My Life Strewn
in cobwebbed attics with childhood toys
and stained photos of smiling girls
before real life began and smiles ran dry.

My Life Strewn
in boxes opened only when memory stirs or
fails to remember some important date
important no more.

My Life Strewn
with memories of a time before you
beckoned me across the sky.
For now, my life contained.

# Wooden Crosses on the Back Road to Vegas

wooden crosses at the side of the road
tell all and nothing of lives un-lived,
dreams cut short, shards of metal, flying glass.

Did you see mist blanket the hills, hawk soar high?
Did morning's warmth make you feel good to be alive?
Did you see death standing round that bend and know?

Mothers, fathers, daughters, sons,
empty houses, crowded graves,
wooden crosses keep your secrets now.

# Slouching Toward Mt. Rubidoux Manor

## INLANDIA CREATIVE WRITING WORKSHOP - RIVERSIDE
## LED BY RUTH NOLAN

### CONTRIBUTORS

Pierce J. Boulet, Celena Diana Bumpus, Mike Cluff,
Carlos Cortés, Laurel Cortés, Amy Floyd,
Michelle Gonzalez, Joan Koerper, Timothy Perez,
Mike Sleboda, Diana Twiss, Mae Wagner,
J. Ladd Zorn, Jr.

PIERCE J. BOULET

## Gracious Living in the Inland Empire

Growing up in the low down
SoCal, the only place
I ever saw the seasons change
was the classroom bulletin board.

      Snow men fallen
already assembled.
      Multicolored tulip rows
bypassing bulbs.
      Cornucopias
spouting co-opted
grocery store creations.

All
purported reflections
of the season at hand.


But I did have the crickets!

Cricking in tandem

starlight's twinkle.


      And for awhile......
      I had my dad.

Who taught me all manner of flora
and some fauna, within the confounds
of our empire's nativity.

Hibiscus and Bottlebrush, crimson in clover.

Furry loquats boasting more seed than fruit.
Birds of Paradise  s t r a i n i n g  for
lift off.
Humming and other

competently
launched birds.


Bougainvillea showcasing
fuchsia with climbing.
A beloved stray cat we
immediately named Ours.


The prolific, and poisonous if eaten, (which
the red headed hellion from across the street did
and had to have her stomach pumped)
White
and pink Oleander.


He was the Tin Man
needing a heart, his
fevered rheumatically
beyond repair.


Offering himself up
to 1960s technology,
which was not as yet
advanced enough
to do the trick.


He returned
to the earth and the stars
expanding our empire.


Cricking me
light and lullabies


Delineating
my seasons.

# A Gift Given

I re-call who I came to be this time.
It was so clear when I stepped out of the threshold circle.
All my previous selves were there, cheering me on.
Forthcoming ones were present too.

It was so clear when I stepped out of the threshold circle.
Purpose and passion moved me on.
Forthcoming ones were present too.
Somewhere along the way, I forgot.

Purpose and passion moved me on.
They are buried in a body now.
Somewhere along the way, I forgot.
I'll never forget my breath buried in Fai's neck.

They are buried in a body now.
My senses cheer - yes yes yes!
I'll never forget my breath buried in Fai's neck.
Breathing her in I came full circle.

My senses cheer - yes yes yes!
In that sweet breath were all here present.
Breathing her in I came full circle.
It's as if I never left.

In that sweet breath were all here present.
Embodied in a gift given.
It's as if I never left.
I re-call who I came to be this time.

# Pollyanna Fucks the Sun

I told my mom I'd be there around 3:00, but here it was 3:27 and I was still poring over the buckets full of roses at the local grocery. *Just relax*, I cajoled, as I rummaged through the colorful offerings. Enjoy your visit, everything will be fine. My disquietude had nothing to do with running late or which flowers to choose. It was the news I had to share with Mom that concerned me.

*Which to choose?* I was partial to the light pink with pale green tips. The oval sticker read Chablis.

*I think I may have brought those the last time,* I thought, *or maybe the time before.*

The red roses were too common, although with a name like *Rouge Baiser* they would be fun to announce when presenting them to my mom. She always got a kick out of reading the sticker and enunciating the name in her dramatic fashion. After examining the contents of each bucket, I decided on the variegated gold and red ones, dubbed….. "drum roll please" *Rumba!* "Let's get ready to ruuuuum-ba!" I chanted in cadence to the iconic boxing preamble, *Let's get ready to ruuuuumble.*

My relationship with my mother, over the years, had been a rumba: complex, passionate, percussion-driven, lots of emotional push and pull, recoil and reconciliation. We were currently basking in a period of mutual adoration, and I was curious to see how this visit might impact the next steps of our precarious promenade.

Every month or so I made the ninety-minute trek from my job in Burbank to my childhood home in Riverside, CA, to the house my parents purchased the year before my birth. Daddy died when I was ten but Mom and her four cats still occupied the five-bedroom, tract home estate.

I drove up the Magnolia-lined street and pulled into the driveway. Roses in hand, I rang the doorbell. I heard my eighty-year-old year old mother shuffle along the wood floors, and then her high pitched, rhetorical, "Who's there?"

She greeted me in a hot pink outfit, in magnificent contrast to her silver hair. When I handed her the bouquet, she feigned her usual 'you shouldn't have' expression of surprise.

"Ruuuuumba" I trumpeted, shaking my hips and pointing to the sticker.

I gave her a hug and disappeared down the hall to my old bedroom, leaving her to cut and arrange the flowers. After depositing my bags, I headed for the fridge, hoping for some delectable leftover.

I was rarely disappointed and this time was no exception. The top shelf hosted a white styrofoam box messy with tender beef ribs smothered in Gram's secret sauce, accompanied by an ample scoop of mac & cheese. Transferring the contents to a plate, I nuked the spoils and joined Mom at the table.

This was our usual ritual: roses, refreshment, and some good old familial 'chewing the fat' at the dining room table.

At my mother's elbow was a nearly complete Press Enterprise crossword puzzle. The challenging puzzle, she liked to remind me, not the simpleton version in the entertainment section. Whenever I visited, she shared the few blank boxes that had somehow circumvented her well-endowed cerebral synapses. She was always impressed when I was able to spit out some morsel from my disparate well of knowledge and aid her in filling out the puzzle.

After hearing the litany of home repairs required since my last visit, and after having been duly chastised for not properly acknowledging the cats, my fingers and plate licked clean, our conversation turned to the Bill Maher show that had aired the night before.

"He pronounces controversy, Con-TRAUV-er-see," my mom said, "just like Kiki used to say."

I couldn't believe it. I hadn't been there more than fifteen minutes and here was a perfect segue into the subject I had hoped to broach sometime during my visit. Did I dare run with it? Before Mom could steer the conversation away, I blurted out, "Speaking of conTRAUVersee..."

My mother's eyes widened. Then her body stiffened as if bracing herself. She was used to my disconcerting tendency to drop bombs out of the blue, as if they were mere raindrops sent to bless their recipients. I'd been dropping them ever since I was a teenager. Now fifty, it struck me that not much had changed.

"What?" she asked, cringing, as if preparing for a blow.

"I'm seeing a woman I really like." Swallow, grin.

"What!" she demanded, contorting her face. "You've never shown any inclination that way before!"

"I've always loved women, Ma" I laughed, trying to quell the tsunami roiling inside me. "Jim and I used to check out women together all the time."

Just the mention of my ex-husband was usually enough to send her into a diatribe of his failings.

But here she sat, speechless. If she could have blamed him, she would have, but she was preoccupied with the matter at hand.

"At first I thought I was bi-" I continued. "But then I thought, no, I'm pan-sexual because I love the whole gamut: the benter the gender the better."

She raised an eyebrow and leaned back in her *Oh this is going to be good* pose. I continued enthusiastically.

"Then I realized, what I really am is omni-sexual because I love everything—the natural world, the trees, the wind, the..."

Lurching forward in her chair, confident that she had me now, she demanded, "So, what are you going to do, FUCK the sun? What about that, huh? Burn yourself up?"

Relieved to have divulged my news but still running on adrenalin, I smiled. I sat quietly, allowing time for her ridiculous comment to settle in. I loved my mother's wit, her passion, her droll sense of humor. It also helped that she didn't have a homophobic bone in her body and that I had long since learned not to take her cutting criticism too personally.

She leaned back and gazed away, feigning detachment.

"So," she asked, "is she a card carrier?"

I took this to mean, *has she been lesbian all her life?* (Although today, several years after this conversation, and upon further reflection, I wonder if she was asking, in her own way, whether this woman was a militant dyke, someone who had used her wiles to beguile this gullible daughter of hers and recruit her into the 'lifestyle'.)

"Yep," I replied, "she's never been with a man."

Mom smirked, as if to say, *surprise, surprise*, but her affect belied an empty victory.

"It's just that life is hard enough and, (heavy sigh), I don't want it to be any harder for you than it already is."

I listened sympathetically, nodding. I wasn't about to inflict my Pollyanna perspective on how the world had changed, and how the younger generation was so much more open and accepting.

Or my notion that those who came before had taken the brunt of discrimination, paving the way for contemporary queers everywhere.

You have to understand: my mom was a card carrier herself, of another variety. She was a longtime member of the Skeptic's Society, regularly attending society lectures and the annual symposium at Cal Tech, one of my father's alma maters. She read *Skeptic*, the quarterly magazine, cover to cover and kept every issue. I knew enough to protect myself from the incredulity and sarcasm I would have had to endure, had I confessed that it was my experience that people loved being around love. And that when Teri and I walked around holding hands in our conservative, white bread, sterile, planned community, folks were happy for us because they could see how much we loved each other.

Blinded by love as I was, I am glad I had the sense to keep quiet. Pollyanna eventually did fuck the sun, but, sorry Ma, having tasted the fruit, there's no turning back for this girl.

As our latest round of rumba was coming to a close, I told my mom that I wanted her to meet Teri. She alluded to her suspicion that this was just another phase, another harebrained idea her la-la-land daughter was throwing herself into, and conceded that she did not want to meet the card carrier.

Mom and Teri never met. We broke up after an intense, four-month romance.

I waited several days before telling Mom. It was during my break at work, walking the perimeter of the office parking lot, which is when I usually called her. After I delivered the news, the line went silent, and then her voice, gentle with genuine sympathy, responded, "I'm sorry to hear that. I know she meant a lot to you."

# Riverside

Like a stuttering lightbulb
Our sun flickers
Blows out
"Invaders have left us in darkness"
Our electricity
a weak flashlight
in the total midnight
that remains
We stand together
In stunned silence
Frozen
Heart beats frantic
threatening to escape
from the cavity of our chests
Beyond our comprehension
We do not think yet
of adapting
adjusting
living in this environment noir
Instead we stand
Reassuring breaths measured
by each other
Drawing us closer
Through the obsidian night
Until we clutch our hands
desperately
crushing
Like two small children
knowing our parents
will not arrive in time
We've got to take action
ourselves

# She Had a Thing for Dolphins II

*Though she lived in the low desert*
*of the Inland Empire.*
*She had a thing for dolphins.*
*Because they reminded her*
*of her former life on the coast.*
*Growing up on the Puget Sound,*
*in the city of Seattle.*
*Dolphins came to represent*
*her talisman,*
*her spirit guide,*
*her grounding stability,*
*her courage to leave her land*
*of multicultural integration and freedom*
*to resettle in a completely different land.*
*One of a unclear purpose or agenda.*
*As a result she integrated her optimistic nature*
*into her a philosophy that allowed her*
*to accept and integrate into her new city*
*in the southern California desert.*
*As well as, deepening her sense*
*of self-awareness*
*and her perceived vulnerabilities*
*as described in her spiritual and*
*emotional connection to dolphins.*

She has a thing for dolphins
who dance on the waves
who chatter in response to greetings
swim with her in the ocean
eat fish for snacks from her hands
laugh at her jokes
leap in the moonlight
gleam on her wrists
shine on her fingers

She liked dolphins

She has a things for dolphins
who see everything
and tell nothing
who nudge to be cuddled
help her to shore when she is tired
sleep while they swim
in the safety of the night
who find comfort
sleeping next to their mommies
after having bad dreams
She likes dolphins

She has a thing for dolphins
who are afraid
of being alone in the world
have no brothers or sisters
who knit shrugs for strangers
make beautiful charm jewelry
from sparkling dolphin charms
who make friends easily
who have survived breast cancer
who bear their scars with pride
whose friends build beach houses
listen carefully to lyrics in songs
knowing some songs
speak directly to her
who wear only knee skirts
who have no allergies
She likes dolphins

She has a thing for dolphins
who prefer silent times alone
are tired of making others laugh
on command
who look cute when they are angry
who deep in their hearts
are shy of strangers
She likes dolphins

MIKE CLUFF

# Riverside, July 2013

Coming like a storm
the freed water
ballasts up
the old trailer
in Mona McGee's
back forty,
resettles it
near the Mission Inn entrance
next to a Jaguar and a Cadillac:
she was soon pissed
the city increased her taxes
so much....

after so many years
of equilibrium,
but declared her steel haven hogan
a quaint remnant
the early fifties run amuck.

So now,
she owes tens of thousands
but is allowed to sleep
in a state landmark
never free of charge.

Yesterday is better
and tomorrow she prays,
yearns for another gullywasher
to arrive undiminished force
gather her up
deposit her in Huntington
or Hermosa Beach.

She has always planned
to die with the ocean
within easy view
reach.

# Norco Poem # 11, June 2008

Off the main path
using an abacus for math
in a fly-blown old Norco town
Jean Paul  put the stylus down
began to loudly moan
enough to crack open every stone,
"here on Old Hamner Road
adobe makes many an abode
but the trail of the mighty horse
is now a rutted, brier-ridden, mucky course,
time has moved into a newer century
I consider it a foul penitentiary."

The moon rims above his ice-planted lawn
listens to his bitching without a yawn,
yet the river bluffs are starchly the same,
ignoring the silliness and drama of human change.

# Belgrade

Professor Harold Fudgeson suddenly realized that he had screwed up big time.

The impassive grey-uniformed Yugoslavian customs agent assessed the white powder in the baggie he had extracted from Fudgeson's meticulously-packed, brown-tweed suitcase. The soft crinkling of the baggie echoed throughout the cavernous pre-dawn Belgrade Airport, virtually empty except for the other passengers on Fudgeson's October, 1984, flight from Amsterdam. And, of course, except for the three agents who now hovered around Fudgeson's bag.

Fudgeson fiddled with the knot on his blue-and-white military striped tie. "I can explain," he said with a wan smile, then proceeded with his lecture only to be met by blank stares. "You speak English, don't you? English? None of you speak English?"

The Philosophy professor clumsily loosened his tie and began to demonstrate. With his right hand he dropped the invisible white powder into the glass shape of his left hand, then drank it thoroughly, his head tilted back until he could see the forbidding beams of the airport's drab ceiling. Placing both hands alongside his lips, he traced the flow of the imaginary liquid down his throat, through his chest, then around his hips to his buttocks. The agents showed no sign of comprehension.

By that time more passengers were lining up. With no customs agent to attend to them, all eyed the broadly gesturing professor.

"Did you pack this bag yourself?"

Elation filled Fudgeson at the sound of English coming from the dark-suited functionary who had now joined the ceremony. But elation quickly gave way to concern as Fudgeson realized the import of his questions.

"Yes, I packed it myself."

"Did anyone give you something to put in your bag?"

"No, no. Of course not. I would never do that!"

The baggie had now reached the functionary, who smelled the contents, touched the powder with his finger, and then placed a dab on the tip of his tongue.

"Look, here's what happened."

Fudgeson tried to keep his narrative uncustomarily short. How he had to bring so much stuff for the conference in Dubrovnik. How he had tried to save space in his suitcase by removing things from their containers and scrupulously measuring a week's supply into each baggie. That he was very, very sorry for any confusion he had caused.

Two blue-uniformed guards arrived, sporting guns and hand-cuffs. They nodded unsmilingly as the functionary showed them Fudgeson's passport, then placed it inside his black briefcase.

In desperation, Fudgeson turned to the growing crowd of spectators. Frantically ripping the tie from his neck, he waved it wild-ly and shouted, "Please everybody, please listen. Can anybody help me? I know this is going to sound crazy, but do any of you happen to have a container of Metamucil in your suitcase?"

Silence. "I just need the container, please. I'll be glad to pay you for it."

Fudgeson heard, at least he hoped he heard, the sound of a suitcase being unzipped. Then he spotted a smiling woman reaching into her bag.

# The Man in the Polyester Tam-O-Shanter

The streets became a parking lot.
No movement could be seen.
Nobody gave you half an inch
When lights went red to green.

And then the monster came along
And everybody knew
That it was time to give some space
To let the monster through.

Its tam-o-shantered driver
With spectacles so thick
His shoulders hunched above the wheel
His wobbling wheel so quick

His gray hair sticking through his ears
His polyestered cap
His loving purple-headed wife
Is trying to read the map.

Yet on it comes without a pause
A terrifying sight
The driver staring straight ahead.
He looks not left, not right.

The monster wiggles back and forth
It knows not where it goes.
At least that's what the others think
'Cause only Tam-O knows.

No beast so fierce that spreads more fear
Than seniors at the wheel.
Than Tam-O on a graying head
That makes his tires squeal.

I watched in awe as he pushed through
As others gave him space.
The others might be young and quick
But Tam-O won the race.

I watched with fear and envy
But learned a lot that day
Of polyestered tam-o power
That always clears the way.

So now that I'm a senior
Unruly head of gray
I never fear of traffic jams.
I know the game I'll play.

'Cause I've got tam-o-shanter
Who rides with me each day.
He's resting on the seat by me.
He's waiting till I say.

"I see it's gridlock time again.
It's time for us to play.
It's time to frighten younger creeps.
Let's you and I make hay."

And when he climbs aboard my head
I hunch and stare and bite.
I gently wiggle steering wheel.
The car jerks left and right.

And then, as if by magic,
The other cars depart
And give me space to slither through
While cursing this old fart

Who never should be driving
Who ought to take the bus
Who shouldn't be behind the wheel
Whose antics make them cuss.

Then tam-o-shanter goes to bed.
He's done his daring deed.
He's shown them polyester power
That age can conquer speed.

I won't leave home without him.
I'll show those younger jerks
That tam-o-shanter rules the world.
He's one of aging's perks.

They may be young and virile
Their faces firm and fine.
But I've got tam-o-shanter
The last laugh now is mine.

# Portrait

It's a portrait of my high school band onstage in the Oceanside-Carlsbad Union High School auditorium. My mother made copies of the picture to distribute to her daughters and a few of our friends. I am seated front and center (behind the podium, of course) with my bass clarinet and in my horrible pea-green band uniform. My sister Gloria is in the trumpet section, and all of the friends I hung out with, "the band kids," are in that wide, (thankfully) black and white portrait.

I can still recite my band kids' names, even after almost sixty years. I often look at their faces, trying not to think of how many of them are gone now, and to me they are all—vividly—seventeen.

# AMY FLOYD

## Bird Lady

"Hey, you mind if I get a drink of water from your hose ma'am?" the old man asked. He'd been pushing a stolen shopping cart full of cans and bottles down the street when he paused to wipe the sweat off his face with the front of his shirt. He looked tired and hot and I knew he was thirsty.

I shrugged and he came closer, eyeing the house like it was about to jump on him and tear him limb from limb.

"You live in the bird lady's house, don't ya?" The old man asked me.

I nodded. I had heard it called that before, but hadn't known why. "I'll give you a beer if you tell me more about it." I said.

He looked up at the house again, pulling the cart along beside him like a stubborn mule. He sighed and started in.

"She was a crazy one."

"I kind of thought that what with you calling her the 'bird lady'", I said. "Nothing ever good comes from being named after an animal. 'Cat lady', 'dog lady' you name it. It conjures the image of a house overrun with refuse and tons of animals kept in cages or running around the house. And the person in charge of the chaos being more of a mess in his or her head than in the house."

"Yeah, well" the man said. "She was a real nut job."

"How so?" I asked.

"She treated crows and sparrows like they were her children. I came by once and she was even feeding a pigeon with a spoon out of her bowl of cereal like it was a kid or something. She was kissing it and petting it." He made a face and stuck out his tongue.

I laughed at the image and he scowled at me, sneering up into the sky. He edged away, but the promise of a beer brought him back a few steps later. "So how about that brew?" he asked.

"Tell me more. You get the beer when I get to know more about this place."

"Nuh-uh." He shook his head. "You go get it for me and then I'll tell you more."

138

Just then a crow flew over the house and its shadow passed between us.

"Nu-huh. I'm outta here, man. You can keep the beer. Feed it to the damned crows. Place ain't never been the same with them ever since she'd gone."

The man shuffled off into the heat of the day, still parched since he'd never gotten that drink from the hose or the promised beer.

The crow watched him leave with black oil-drop eyes and cawed a warning at his back. Then it turned to me and I had the urge to follow the old man's advice and pour the beer into a bowl and leave it out on the lawn to reward the bird for its trouble.

# The Ring

I found it on the floor when I was seven and playing make-believe in the spare bedroom down the hall.

A gold ring, pitted and scarred, was curled up in the palm of my hand like a tiny shining salamander.

My mother had been moving boxes around in the closet all week, looking for things to give away to charity, bagging old clothes that no longer fit, wrapping old knick knacks in tissue paper and tying up forgotten magazines in bundles. All had been left in the driveway the night before, large dark huddled figures that sprawled across the front of the house, only to be gone the following morning, leaving no prints of their escape in the dew upon the grass.

But like magic, the ring was here. It stayed and caught my eye as I wandered the newly opened spaces of the dark room, pretending that the closet was a cave and that I was an explorer.

A ring that glinted in the ray of my tiny flashlight. My heart leaped. Was this really magic? Where had it come from? Was it meant for me? If I put it on my finger, would it magically transport me to a fairy land?

I hid it away with my other treasures: pretty rocks, dried flowers and other odd bits I collected while I played 'Adventurer'.

Many years later, when taking my box of Treasures from the same closet that seemed destined to hold old memories for the family, My mother looked inside and threw the box from her as if it contained something poisonous.

Mom, what's wrong? I asked, looking at her hand, her white face. Had a spider crawled from the storage box and bitten her? "Are you hurt?" I looked for the bite.

"That!" She yelled. "That thing -where did you get that thing?!"

I looked to the floor, hoping to find what had offended her. Just rocks, a few seashells and leaves nestled in the brown carpet. And there, glinting in the light was my golden friend, the ring.

"Where did you get that?!" she yelled and left the room.

It was only a ring, I told myself. And all at once it became something more. Men's clothes lumped in bags and left at the curbside long ago. Pictures in photo albums thrown into the garbage. A smiling man I would never know. A man who still haunted my mother.

# Pride Revisited

We sit alone in the car
waiting for the sparks to start.
9pm hits and the music begins.
Same songs they played last year,
yes, god bless America from
sea to shining sea.

Between the far away palm trees
we see the red, whites, and blues
with some orange and purples mixed in.

The music ends but the sparks continue
for a minute or two after.
Surprisingly, we do not see
the typical red glow of fire
on Rubidoux Mountain.

we return to our small home
and on the television I see
Macy's begins their firework show,
(which I never knew they had one.)
A few minutes later my eyes
start to close and I go to bed thinking,
am I still proud to be an America?

# The Warrior Writes

Like a warrior
refusing to revisit the battlefield
I plead the images
and sensations remain buried.
Refusing,
they bubble to the surface
easing the lid
oozing slowly
through the cracks
of the aged oak barrel
fermented
releasing
demanding
I write.

Like a sprite
time traveling though billions
of galaxies, twirling
in fluorescent circling ripples
with spiral galaxies,
conjuring the birth of new stars,
skipping on ancient stars of
elliptical galaxies, and merging
with irregular nebulas
uncovering new worlds
joy bursts from my heart.
I write.

Like a monk of old
scurrying over scratches and pen strokes
engaging in a sacred, visual art,
once reserved for a chosen few,

none of them women,
quill in hand
I write.

143

# The Clay of My Soul

I am a potter
listening to
ancient souls
singing in the clay
the wet, malleable
substance of
Creation
swirls counterclockwise
in my hands
opening, pulling,
stretching
taking form and shape
transforming
with every sensual,
sensuous, loving
living touch
connecting me
with all who have
come before,
and All That Is,
transforming
the clay of my soul
delightfully dancing
in synchronized grace
merging with Mystery.

# Mountain Sunrise

Careening down
6,750 feet of narrow
rugged, ribboned roads
from Big Bear
the sun dips behind
Mt. San Gorgonio
only to appear again
beckoning a new morning
sunrise after sunrise.
Peeking.
Teasing.
Disappearing.
Reappearing.
Awakening.
Refreshing.
Until,
rounding the last curve
to the San Bernardino Valley floor
it transmutes into
an unrelenting
blazing
erupting
death-defying
dueling warrior.

# Pure Gold Homeless

## I

The well-dressed man
in a gray pin-striped suit and tie
and worn polished shoes
stands with the group
of migrant workers
outside the home improvement store
at Madison and Indiana.
"I was laid off," he says.
"My unemployment ran out.
I have a family to feed.
Is there any work you can give me?
Please?"

## II

The homeless man
stands in the middle of
Fairmount Boulevard
spinning in circles
gesticulating and yelling
at unseen demons
trying to pick
devil dust out of his hair
that rained down on him,
along with other body parts,
in Vietnam.

## III

Eyes wide with shock,
the stocky man with tear streaked
cheeks, rivers through soot,
clutches
his wife in her jeans and boots

and their four children,
in a huddle,
pointing to their two horses,
three dogs and two cats.
"We were able to get us
and the animals out," he says.
This Old Fire got everything else.
Everything we owned in the world."


IV
Crouching in
her Santa Ana riverbed camp,
on a red and black checkered blanket,
three gallons of water in plastic bottles
next to the toilet paper,
the homeless woman
presses her two sleeping children
tightly against her
tattered black cotton jacket,
hyper-vigilant to the
sounds of night:
prowling coyotes,
packs of wild dogs,
men high on drugs,
crazy as a night bug,
teens in gang initiation rituals
eager to add fresh wounds
to the scars that already
tattoo her body and soul.

# The Sheep-Herder's Angels

Gripping the steering wheel so tightly my knuckles glow neon yellow, I gun the accelerator. Spitting up rotting citrus peels and gravel, the rear tires of my Subaru GL10 clear the orange grove bouncing off railroad tracks seconds ahead of the Southern Pacific locomotive barreling toward the crossing at Alessandro and San Timoteo Canyon Road. The carefully calculated risk is too close for comfort even if it does shave twenty minutes off my morning commute. Snaking my way through the once-ancient riverbed, I turn south up into the pass on Redlands Boulevard and reach the stop sign right before the entrance to the I-60 West. I'm the last of four cars and two pick-up trucks, sitting in-wait.

Moreno Valley, bordered on the north and south by undulating hills, emits that sense of calm that miles of working ranches generate, disguising the harsh landscape of the Badlands to the east and the washboard, thirsty roads that lay just beyond the irrigated parcels of green. Mornings, drivers idling at the stop sign wait patiently to turn left down the on-ramp while the weathered, stoop-shouldered sheep-herder with his curved handmade staff, highly efficient herding dogs and flock, cross the Redlands Boulevard overpass to the north side where the sheep continue grazing. To me, it's sacred ritual honoring a simpler time in Southern California, offering an early morning respite, like a 6 a.m. Mass. We wave, or nod, at the old man in the large sombrero passing like a priest in his brightly woven poncho vestments, nodding blessings in return.

Cutting the engine, I run my hands down the center of my blouse and skirt smoothing out the wrinkles starting to form under the seatbelt. A quick glance in the rear view mirror assures me I am presentable. Settling in, I review case notes for an 8 a.m. court appearance.

Spotting the black Ford SUV speeding to a screeching halt behind me, sends waves of unease washing over my toes, entering thirsty cells and seeping up to my entrails, pooling in my gut like unwanted globulin. The fool on my bumper torques his vehicle;

148

revving his engine. A suburban sleezebag caught in some delusion that he's at the start line of the Riverside International Raceway waiting for the flag to go down. Laying on the horn he pulls to my left, missing my tail light by an inch, trying to get ahead in the oncoming lane before being waived back. Slamming the car in reverse, narrowly avoiding hitting those of us in queue, he ends up, once again, kissing my tailpipe. Through his open driver's side window he's bellowing obscenities orchestrated with matching gesticulations. I'm praying again; this time for self control. Too late. I've had it with this obnoxious obstreperous outsider. Everyone in line knows you don't cause consternation to the sheep and dogs by carrying on and making noise.

Curling the fingers of my left hand around the driver's side car door handle I start to pull it forward when a flash of movement interrupts. One of the drivers ahead is easing out of his green Toyota. Carefully unfolding his lanky body he hooks both hands in his belt tugging up his pants then motions to the other drivers. Just one slight nod of the head is all it takes.

Slowly releasing my fingers from the door handle I'm watching every movement with sentry precision. The car doors sound like a well orchestrated brass band sequence as they open then slam shut in timed progression.

The young blond in the white painting overalls, biting his lip and flexing his hands into fists, looks no more than twenty. A second man, with striking white hair, wearing indigo blue jeans and a blue and green checkered shirt, oozing charisma in his eyes, is moving with the grace of a dancer and the bearing of a person in charge. The red-haired driver stands only five-foot-four, but, his celery green silk suit and tie, and soft brown Italian leather shoes, reek of power. The man in the brown suit and shoes would be unexceptional except for his garish Hawaiian sunset tie in yellows, greens and oranges. The driver of the white Dodge Ram pick-up, easily six-foot-five wearing a Western cut white, red and black shirt with snap cuffs, tight black jeans, and a cowboy hat with a pony tail slithering down his back, is the last to join the group.

I can't take my eyes off them. One by one they pass within a breath of my rearview mirrors, not even noticing me, focusing only on the man in the black Ford SUV. Slipping behind the boot of my car the men block my view.

For once in my life, I decide to stay put. I carried a gun as a police detective in a major mid-western city, not that long ago, but that was behind me. Whatever was going to happen here didn't need my two cents. For the second time that morning I'm sitting white-knuckled at the wheel, biting the inside of my bottom lip, fighting off the adrenalin-driven urge to fly out the door and get into the thick of it. Luckily, a nebulous substance I later thought of as psychological glue affixes me to my seat. Cranking up my Manheim Steamroller tape, drowning out any semblance of the confrontation going on six feet from my rear bumper, I lower my eyes, committed to self-preservation.

The report rips the wind.

Considering the results, everything goes down quickly, smoothly, quietly and without further incident. Slipping back to their cars the men nod respectfully at the sheep-herder as he ambles by. So do I. Then, one by one, each vehicle turns left onto the I-60 ramp merging into the stream of traffic swiftly carrying us back to our daily lives.

***

Last Sunday, the byline of an article in the Riverside *Press-Enterprise* read, "Moreno Valley Death Still Baffles RSO." Recounting the facts of the strange incident of July 22, 1985, the Riverside Sheriff's Office Detectives admitted to being completely stumped about the circumstances surrounding the black Ford SUV found on Redlands Boulevard that auspicious day. The driver was shot once with his own weapon. Speculation was rampant. Was it a suicide? If so, why would the man choose that location of all places? Pleas had circulated for any witnesses. No one came forward.

There were no stoplights or cameras perched on metal supports rapidly recording the license numbers of cars waiting at the stop sign. No glossed-over eyes peering out from one of the hundred thousand bedroom windows that later occupied the valley. No cell phones to record the events. Any footprints or tire impressions there might have been obliterated by the sheep's hooves and a fierce windstorm that hit just before the RSO arrived at the scene. Trace evidence was gleefully carried by dust devils, tumbleweed, dried sagebrush and debris to the Badlands and beyond. The only fingerprints on the gun were that of the driver of the SUV. DNA testing was practically non-existent even when there was data.

I have yet to recognize any of the other cars, or drivers, involved in that fateful event. Not that I want to. Okay, I admit, I do keep my eye open for that man in the indigo jeans with the pressed blue and green checkered shirt whom I found so appealing. So far, *nada*.

## Silver Fish

my mouth will swallow me whole
one day—i am no good.

put me on the spot—i'll give you
aaaalllll up.

i could never make it as a spy.
even if i were a good liar

i'd tattle-tell on myself.
i'd see me in the mirror,

 slap my hand, hard,
over the me's mirror mouth

myself trying to get it all out of me.
the words scurrying like silver fish

through the gaps of mine's fingers.
and i would smash them—my voice

escaping from powdery remains
in muffled gasps leaving gray smudges

like fingerprints.

# Super Man

They ate bad frosties from Wendy's. Both ended
up at the E.R to control the flow of various fluids
that seemed to spew simultaneously from both ends
of them. The liver and kidneys were fine. It'll pass,
the doctor said.

It was Hollow's Eve, so when I tried to explain
to him why we weren't going he just looked at me—
a thin dog that hadn't eaten in a while: eyes
sunken in, ribs protruding, something clicked
in his throat, as if the skin needed to be lubricated
with water or love or both.

And he said in a sort of whisper, Let's go Poppa.
Let's go. You said, Poppa. You said.
It's near impossible rationalizing with a three-year
old. He was already potty trained, but I wrapped
the biggest diaper on him I could find.

Put him in a pair of Cheetos-stained black sweats,
his favorite Thomas the Train long sleeve, and stuffed
his favorite blanket down into the neck of that worn
tee-shirt best I could, stuffed tiny feet into oversized
slippers, grabbed two plastic grocery bags: one for puke,
the other for candy, told the wife, One time around the block.

She held her hand over her mouth, gulped something back
down. I promised, I said. She nodded and quickly retreated.
We went around that block twice. He was the saddest looking
super hero on the block. But I believe when the time comes
he'll be there to catch me when I fall.

# July 4th, 2012

Her father's rot in his gut had shrunk
just enough.

I figured it was time to go—
we left in a hurry, haphazardly

packing our things, tossing it all
in the trunk, kids and all

leaving in a swirl of dust.
Her father, in his room, struggling

to pop the lid off his fifth set
of pills for the day

the bowl of soup she left
at his bedside gone cold.

And in the middle of that wide
starless sky my fingers began to itch

and I saw the first of them:
sparkly dots, then asterisks, then blooming

onions, cat scans, MRI's, survivor's meetings,
tears.

And the sky blinked as if it had an eyelash
gouging at its multihued orb and without a way

to wash it out—there were no clouds for miles.

# Car Parts and Dreams

It's summer time, when car enthusiasts finally get done putting the final touches on their chariots as they drive them out into the sunlight for the first time to make the annual trek to the local car show circuit. For me, I have a long ways to go to get mine roadworthy again. In my man cave, I see car parts scattered all over the floor. Engine parts piled in boxes. Fenders and door skins hanging precariously on hooks attached to the overhead rafters. I know that someday my car will be finished and I will be able to drive it to the car shows. It's a daunting task, but I'm determined to finish it.

I don't like having to work on my car this way, without a proper place to work on it and the snail-slow progress due to financial constraints. I complain about it all the time. If I ever won the lottery or came into a huge sum of cash, I could dramatically quicken up the pace. As it is, I just have to work on it when I can. Of course, I could never take the easy road and farm out all the work. I will send it out for the major stuff like paint and body work when the time comes, but I'm determined to restore all the little bits and pieces myself. I'm very adept at doing things such as upholstery, plastic repair and cleaning/painting small parts.

If I had a spray booth or even an empty garage, I would attempt to paint it. Some guys have done their own cars that way and their paint jobs have come out amazingly well. The ultimate goal for me is to match the original orange-peel texture, paint thickness and primer overspray from the factory. Whenever I see a perfectly painted car of this vintage, I cringe. It's like a kid's model car that has too much paint on it. They don't seem to look right with perfectly smooth paint unless it's a custom show car or something.

I think about paint jobs a lot. As I walk the car lots, my eyes are drawn to the orange peel surface texture of automobile paint and how it varies from automaker to automaker and even from model to model. Used vehicles are always fun to inspect. I can spot a paint repair twenty feet away. I would make the perfect companion to bring to the lots to inspect a new or used vehicle for previous damage.

155

Maybe I can charge people for this service and make a little side business for myself. Or, I can work as a classic car judge filtering out the bad restorations from the good ones. I don't know if I could handle that, but I certainly have the mindset to do it. Is the factory paint mark at the correct location? Is the paint overspray correctly applied on the firewall? Is the surface thickness of the paint correct? Is that semi-gloss black instead of low-gloss black? Are the warning stickers and labels in the engine compartment positioned in the correct locations? Does the glass have the correct date codes for the year of the car? It's endless what you can judge when it comes to originality.

I'd like to go to the Bloomington Gold Corvette car show one of these days. To win the Bloomington Gold, you'd have to have everything perfect and I mean absolutely perfect in regards to factory stock condition. They actually give seminars on when production changes took effect during the model year to help car restoration enthusiasts win the award. . It's usually the mint original cars that win the award typically. The factory time capsules as they call them. The award is impressive if you win it on a ground-up restoration. In fact, on the older restored Corvettes they judge for this award, they will actually test drive the car it to see if everything functions properly including testing the engine for the correct horsepower and torque curves to see if it's completely stock.

It's a good thing I don't have an older Corvette. Because then, I would agonize over winning the Bloomington Gold award. I'll stick with my Firebird and spend hours upon hours on the web looking at all the factory brochure pictures, car magazine test articles and original never restored cars to base my restoration on. I even found an enthusiast in Great Britain who makes copies of the correct AC Delco label for the original battery. Yeah, I already bought one.

But then again, I don't have to restore it exactly to factory showroom condition. I could get a GM crate 383 fast burn engine and significantly improve performance. I could do an LS2 engine conversion and keep up with newer Mustangs, Camaros and Challengers. A feat the original 235 hp L98 could only dream of. I can always save the original block if I ever decide to sell it someday.

I try to work on the car when I get the chance, depending on my energy levels and funds available. This week, I removed all the rust on the rear sway bar that sat out in the elements for a few years.

Now, I am debating whether to paint it or get it powder coated or just leave it in its natural metal finish to rust again like the factory did. After all the work I did to get the rust off, I think I'll paint it. They sell a particular type of paint that looks like the natural metal finish and it would keep it from rusting again.

I'm grateful that my family had a collection of cars throughout the years to develop and hone my skills in working on cars. It basically started with my uncle's 1977 Oldsmobile Cutlass Supreme where I learned how to perform the basics like car detailing and maintenance similar to what I had learned on my own 1973 Caprice Classic when I turned 18 years old. A few years went by and the muscle car craze began and my uncle purchased a few classic Chevelles and Camaros where I learned how to perform light mechanical repair and restoration work. After that, Corvette fever struck and I had the opportunity to do more complicated mechanical, electrical and restoration work on a few vintage Corvettes he owned.

I want my Firebird to look good when I'm done restoring it.. I want it to look showroom-new like it did back when it was new. I know I will have to remain extremely dedicated to the goal of getting it done. Only then will I be able to enjoy it like I had always wanted. I want to drive it to the local car shows and sit on my folding lawn chair and admire the beauty of the design while I talk to people who are enthusiasts about the same type of car. Well, that's my dream anyway.

# In the Beginning

They'd make eyes at each other in church
but she was wealthy Spanish
and he was of-the-earth Yaqui.

Communion line flirting was all it ever was
or could ever be

until the night he and his banditos
raided a neighboring village—

he opened a dusty trunk and found a wedding dress.

That's when he decided to get his bride.

I don't know how he pulled it off.
They say she wasn't
Unwilling.

He rode off with her in the Harvest moon,
the horse sweating and glistening in the moonlight.

There are pictures of them, barefoot,
toes spread into the soft dirt.

She loved to garden and they made their way
to the groves of Corona.

She buried seeds and sprouted children—
sixteen.

Her brothers finally found her but she was happy
and had laid her roots, like braids.

They brought her a trunk of clothes and her piano.

My grandmother was one of the sixteen children
and she learned the secrets of dancing with the earth
and making green things grow.

She and my grandfather met at the church fair.
After he saw her, he had to know her.

He'd heard her family had gone to Fresno for the Harvest season.
He paid some buddies in beer and cigarettes
for a ride North in the back of a pickup.

Antonia and Raul
Antonia and Raul

Like a couple from a novella—
hot and fiery.

Before he went to Korea
they bought a small home in a new development in Riverside—

La Sierra: a swathe leveled and planted with homes like bright jewels
in a dusty sea.

Within two weeks of their moving in,
the neighbors had started a petition to "get the Mexicans
out of the neighborhood."

But, as my great-grandparents had done, they dug their feet
into the soft earth

and bloomed.

# Letter Home

If we stay, we cannot be together.

There was no thought, really.
No time.

He came to my window that night
and I went with him.

It wasn't until we were sure we'd lost them,
until we approached the border,

that I thought about my parents, my brothers,
and what I'd be leaving behind.

I didn't care about money or status.
I remembered Lupita, my mother's sister,

wearing a hole in the rug, pacing,
and cursing her husband, who'd died.

I wanted love like that—love
that made you insane with longing.

As we crossed over, I imagined my family.

My father, drunk with my brothers,
yelling and cursing and making vows of murder.

And I imagined my mother:
her cheeks tear-stained

she'd stand, staring out the window
absently brushing out her long dark hair.

She'd get the scissors next and cut it
to the nape of her neck

to mourn the loss of her only daughter.
In church, they'd cross themselves

and sing hymns and lift prayers
for the day of my safe return

but at night, my mother would take
her place by the window.

She'd stroke her growing hair,
and hum to fill the ache in her chest.

# Memorial Day

They say he'd wake up screaming
sweat crawling down the sides of his face.

Before Korea, he'd worked the fields and factories.
In the war, he and a partner manned a bazooka.

He'd load it and pray the shell would miss.

After, the walls at home were too white
and the children's laughter made his head ache.

He pulled up grandma's irises
because he hated the slender slope of their leaves.

He worked late and drank long and demanded
the kids call him "Father."

At night, he'd sit in the hot kitchen,
the light buzzing above his dark head.

He'd work math problems and constellations on napkins,
his pen clawing at the dark for innocence.

Today he sits at the same table, eating his ice cream.
First the pink layer, then the brown, then the white.

He palms the wall as he shuffles past, and pauses at the pictures
scanning the eyes for a glimmer of memory.

He leans at the window, staring out at the irises
long ago replanted.

He falls asleep mumbling prayers, half English, half Spanish—
and wakes, his toothless screams

piercing the night.

# After the War

Gasping, she opened the box, her body
lithe and gliding like a young girl's again,
skirt swirling at her shins.

She grabbed his face, looked into his
eyes—two dark full moons—planted her
lips on his blushing, whiskered cheek.

Her left hand strong and thick. The hand
of a woman who has wrung the necks
of plump, squawking chickens.

The hand of a woman who's pounded
golden lumps of masa into salty deliciousness,
now tender against his skin.

The gift was a gold watch. It was the first
time I had ever seen grandma kiss grandpa.
I was sixteen.

Normally, they spoke harshly to each other
in Spanish, two angry hissing, striking snakes.

My grandmother's nose flaring out at the sides,
the tip, a glistening poison arrow.

She'd hug her chin to her neck, her eyes gnawing
at the space before her: black, narrow, determined
with rage, lips thin and pink and spitting.

My granfather's deadliest weapon: retreat.
He'd yell—his thick accent thick, a mouth filled with tar,

throw up his hands and walk away, back heaving—
a tarp billowed in a breeze.

There's a picture of them as newlyweds: she's fifteen,
he a soldier on his way to Korea;
his arms wrap around her,
her head leans in,
they are both smiling.

When he left, she didn't realize she'd kissed her young husband
goodbye for good. She was pregnant and would amble
across the hot grass to look for his letters
in their shiny black mailbox.

They came rarely, if at all. He returned
with souvenirs: flashbacks and night terrors.
He shouldered them with alcohol,

and sat quiet at the window, chewing chiles.

She built a heart-shaped pond with her hands
and the neighborhood kids sat on sun-kissed

peeling shoulders and squeezed between each other's
grass-stained legs to watch the fish go in.

In the mornings, hair tight in curlers, bandanna—
a cloth crown—hugging her head, she heated the coffee
on the stove, and plowed the steaming innards

of baked potatoes with butter and cinnamon,
and slid them into the pockets of six sleepy-eyed,
school-bound children.

After he left for work at the cheese factory
and the children could be heard laughing
at the schoolyard down the street,

she'd sit at the edge of the pond and watch the orange
and white fish pass each other through the water,
their backs hooking the coolness of the surface,

their mouths groping for bugs, and she'd wonder
if they knew each other, if they understood
that they were family.

# Cut the Blossoms

Outside the house the roosters' raucous
caws ricochet off street lights: promises.

In the neighborhood, the boys call out
to the mini-shorted, cascading-bosomed girls;

and pull their starched shirts up by the shoulders
and pinch the crease at the groin of their pants.

Grandma snips the herbs before they flower,
drying the leaves by nailing them—stalks up—
on the beams. "Keeps the roots stretching,"

she says. "Once the flowers open the bees
have at 'em, there's no going back. The plant
becomes bitter and begins to die."

"Anything will grow if you cut it."
One breath: laughs then sighs, snipping stems back,

the gold flecks from the dirt, pulsing
in the brown creases of her hands.

# Our Father

Freeways don't erect themselves,
so when the dusty truck slid up the drive
the boys ran out to carry in his lunch pail and work boots.

If there were only four cans empty on the floor board,
the night might still be good

and the end of his cigar may be all he'd light up.

She never said a bad thing about him,
but sang about her favorite things, in the hall,
as she pulled the weights up on the cuckoo.

On her deathbed, only one spoken regret:
she hadn't married someone else.

A couple nights a week he'd invite the neighbors over.
Jay Grayson told racist jokes over cards.

Dad never laughed but, when the drink was gone,
he recited the conquests of his youth
and slammed the back of his construction-worker hand
against the mouth of anyone close enough to see him.

One August night—a full-moon Thursday—
brother steadied the shotgun against Dad's temple.
Dad snorted and turned in his bed

and the night rang out with silence.

But there was food on the table, clothes on their skins,
and the train whistling in their ears at midnight.

The quiet light—an arm around a tired shoulder
and a gentle nudge against the ear.

The great silence of forgiveness: mysterious in its gravity.

The kids weren't allowed to throw stones:
"Somebody might get hurt gah'damnit."
But they did and when one dove through
the neighbor's slider, the neighbor declared
dad would pay.

But then the truck slid up and Dad's white shirt
gleamed in the sun

and brother explained all that had happened
and the housewives toed the edges of their lawns
and wrung their hands in their aprons
Dad said:

"Is that so?"—and the earth trembled—
"Well,"—the sun snuck behind the clouds—
"Fuck Him!"—and he strolled into the house.

A dog barked.
The kids brought in dad's boots and lunch pail.
There were four empty beers on the floorboard,
and the neighbor never said another thing.

# Riding the Waves

If they were making waves, I was riding them. They were the women in the forefront and I was their cheerleader.

In the 1960s and 70s when my children were young, I wanted the community in which they would grow up to be a good place in which to thrive. I cared about the environment and didn't like mismanaged, runaway growth and pollution. I was on the Jurupa General Plan committee—not once but twice. It was meant to give citizens a voice in how the Jurupa area would be developed; however, it was a discouraging experience on many levels for me. I felt as if my input and that of other citizens was ignored and that it had been a waste of time. Thus, I was grateful for people like former county supervisor Melba Dunlap and activist Penny Newman, both of whom remained active in pursuing goals that I supported.

They, along with Jane Block, Liz Cunnison, Ann McKibben, Sue Nash and Beverly Wingate Maloof, were on the discussion panel of "Making Waves in Inlandia" a joint celebration presented by the Inlandia Institute and the Riverside Metropolitan Museum on March 25, 2011.

I hemmed and hawed about going. It was Sunday. Rain threatened. What if I couldn't find a parking spot near the museum in downtown Riverside? It's not easy for me to walk too far. And in the rain? In the end, I decided I had to go. After all, their history was my history.

When Melba Dunlap campaigned for office, I supported her; she even used a quote from me in her campaign literature. I was glad there could be a woman's voice on the Riverside County Board of Supervisors. It seemed like a bunch of good ol' boys were running the show and they continued to approve too much development in an area that most people wanted to keep semi-rural. That was what surveys had revealed when I was on the Jurupa General Plan. I wanted to be a voice for the little guy but it seemed as if it was the developers and their representatives who had the supervisors' ears. At the meetings, developers had representatives who talked staff and infrastructure when I wanted to talk about quality of life. I was hoping Melba would put the brakes on some of the runaway development.

Ruth Kirkby was an early voice of alarm with regard to the Stringfellow Acid Pits. Toxic waste from all over Southern California was brought to the hills above Glen Avon to a pit which supposedly had an "impermeable clay cap." The fellow who owned the property was named Stringfellow and, unfortunately for him, his name became infamously synonymous with one of the nation's most-toxic waste sites.

Mrs. Kirkby and her husband, Sam, founded the Jurupa Cultural Center off Highway 60, not far from the acid pits. Just as Mrs. Kirkby feared, the clay cap was not impermeable and eventually, a plume of toxic waste washed down into the community of Glen Avon. Penny Newman took on the battle begun by Mrs. Kirkby and has devoted many years of her life to pursuing a cleanup of the pits and advocating for the health and safety of the Glen Avon community. I wrote an editorial about Penny Newman and the Stringfellow Acid Pits which was published on the op-ed page of the Riverside Press-Enterprise on April 30, 2000. My admiration and gratitude for Penny's perseverance and dedication knows no bounds.

Another of my contributions to the op-ed page was published on March 1, 1998, regarding the property of Sam Maloof in Alta Loma. Sam, a world-famous woodworker, had been declared a living treasure by the State of California. (He is now deceased.) I had been to the Maloof home and knew how incredible and historic it was; now it was to be relocated to make way for the 210 freeway. I was crushed. How could this be so?

After the lengthy and involved—but ultimately successful—move, and after Sam's beloved wife, Alfreda, had passed away, Sam married Beverly Wingate. Beverly, who had been active in the Riverside community, was a complement to Sam. She put her touch on the Maloof property, planting native and water-wise plants, turning it into an educational experience for visitors to the estate.

Ruth Anderson Wilson was a frequent subject of local newspaper articles in the '60s and '70s, and I was cheering her on as she fought to preserve areas of the Santa Ana River, among other things. Her delightful personality came through at the panel discussion as she described how men perceived her activism. They thought she should be home doing dishes and tending to children instead of getting in the way of their plans. Jane Block was another of my heroes as she advocated for preserving open space.

But it wasn't only open space and environmental issues that I cared about—I cared about local treasures like the Mission Inn and Fox Theater as well. There were times it looked like neither one would survive; again, there were people within the community who fought to preserve these landmarks.

Yes, I got discouraged—but these women didn't. They fought a good fight, they made waves—and residents of the Inland area can be grateful they did.

I am.

# University Heights Junior High, 1955

It was 1955 and my mother had left my dad for what was to be the last time. Each summer, my mother would load my sister and me in the car and head to California from North Dakota, leaving my dad and two older brothers behind. I'll never understand, as a mother, how she could leave my brothers, starting when all of us were pretty young—but that was life as we knew it.

The other times, it had been temporary. This one was supposed to be for good. She wouldn't just find a job for the summer and earn enough to get us back home in time for the start of school.

My grandmother's family, the Belds, had settled in Riverside sometime in the late '30s or early '40s. They all lived in a radius of a mile or two near the area bounded by what was then Eighth Street and Chicago Avenue. My mother couldn't afford a place of our own so I stayed with my grandma and grandpa, my mother stayed with grandma's sister, Aunt Jane, and my sister stayed with an aunt and uncle. Grandma and Aunt Jane lived near one another on Eucalyptus Avenue and my aunt and uncle lived on 5th Street, next to what was later determined to be a toxic site. Four of five members of their family ultimately died from cancer.

My sister, who was four years younger than I, enrolled in Longfellow Elementary School which was directly across from our grandma and grandpa's house. I would be a ninth grader at University Heights Junior High on Eighth Street and Kansas Avenue, across from the early Delia's Grinders.

I was such a country bumpkin. Quiet, shy and VERY self conscious. I had only about three different outfits to wear and a pair of red flats and maybe a pair of tennis shoes. One of the dresses was yellow—I remember it well. A delicate white flower print against pale yellow and a white dropped waistband. It was fortunate that I loved that dress, since I had to wear it so often—although I don't think it went so well with the red shoes.

My mother's cousin, Viola, lived at the corner of Kansas Avenue and Linden. It was decided that I would accompany Viola's

173

daughter, Barbara, to school, instead of me having to go alone. First days of school can be tough under the best of circumstances and this one would be the hardest ever. Now mind you, I came from a school where all twelve grades had been housed in one building and two cottages on campus. And now I would be going to a school that housed only three grades—seventh, eighth, and ninth. (At the time, Poly was the only high school in Riverside and was located across from the RCC campus. A new Poly was eventually built and RCC expanded into Poly's old space.)

Barbara was adopted and speculated that movie star Ava Gardner was most likely her real mother as she saw a distinct resemblance between her and Ava. Barbara was the exact opposite of me. She wore gypsy hoop earrings, low-cut peasant blouses and skirts cinched with a wide belt. The boys all flocked around her. I had never had a boyfriend, much less a flock of them.

A fellow ninth grader saw me with Barbara and wondered what this country bumpkin was doing with the gypsy girl. Barbara was vivacious and confident. I looked lost and confused. (Incidentally, Barbara grew up, got married and, as far as I knew, was a wonderful wife and mother. Unfortunately, she died of cancer at a young age.)

My new friend, Sandy Kringer, lived in a big old house on Kansas Avenue, across from where Barbara lived. I was lucky Sandy took me under her wing. There were many things I didn't understand about this new school—for instance, ninth graders were the only ones who could use the middle stairs, a perk of being an upperclassman. We had home rooms, a whole new concept for me. And PE was very different than what I had known in North Dakota.

And lo and behold, a boy had a crush on me! In spite of my limited wardrobe and shy personality, I must have appealed to him. He was tall, cute and nice and his name was Marshall. His father was a professor at the newly minted campus of UCR. Marshall's friends were the in-crowd, the popular kids—which was a whole new experience for me. I suspect most of their parents were professional people. His friends would sing "Mae and Marshall, Mae and Marshall, go together like a horse and carriage..." to the tune of "Love and Marriage," a song made popular that year by Frank Sinatra. At the school carnival, Willie the Wolf, the school mascot, "married" us, sealing the deal with a tin-foil ring but no kiss.

Nine weeks into the new school year, my mother decided this wasn't the last time, after all. We would return to North Dakota for two more years, until my brother graduated in 1957. So, back to North Dakota we went and I had a second first day of school that year, which really *was* the hardest ever of my life. I remember standing in the superintendent's office, sobbing, as I looked out the window at the students streaming by who all looked so at home, so secure, so belonging.

In the meantime, the old University Heights campus became the Cesar Chavez Community Center and Bobby Bonds Recreation Center. Eighth Street became University Avenue. Delia's Grinders replaced their original building with a new one—but, fortunately, never replaced the formula for their delicious grinders—and my family is on its fourth generation of being loyal Delia's customers. Although I haven't seen him since way back when, Marshall went on to become a professor at the University of Georgia. My mother, sister and I did return to Riverside in 1957 and two years later, I graduated from Poly High—and, at my high school reunions, I still see some of the kids who sang Mae and Marshall all those years ago—although I doubt that they would remember. And 57 years later, Sandy and I remain friends, the kind of friends who take each other under our respective wings, as needed.

And one of these days—perhaps a day when I just have to have a Delia's ham grinder—I am going to cross the street to the old University Heights Junior High and see if I can walk up those middle school stairs once more.

# J. LADD ZORN, JR.

## Like the Walls of Jericho

Maybe because my attention is always in a book when I walk the track at the high school, so many months passed before tonight, when the edges of a memory came around me, like a déjà vu, and I looked up: I'd been there twenty years earlier. My surprise bordered on amazement. How had I been working there so many months and not recognized the place? It seemed to mean something, and I walked up into the grandstands to sit where I had sat so many years earlier and try to remember.

The ocean had swallowed the sun that day when my room-mate, Barf we called him, and I walked with giddy steps from the house we rented in Newport Beach. A salty breeze flapped our trunks, and a sound like kettledrums flooded the street as the surf boomed along the shore. "I feel like a kid on Christmas morning," I remember saying.

Teeth crowded out the bottom half of Barf's face; he was half a head taller than me, and I imagined Barf's smile bit off his head. "Huh," Barf agreed, and sipped his beer.

We walked down a narrow alley and knocked on a door.

"We come for the fun, Gus," I said when the door opened.

Gus used to gel his hair like bamboo in a tiger trap. "Come in," he said.

His name wasn't really Gus, but I called him Gus because of the fungus. Gus closed the door, and Barf pulled from his pocket a wad of money and handed it to Gus, who disappeared down a hall.

Clownfish floated among anemone tentacles and coral in an aquarium that hummed and bubbled. Humahumanukanuka apu'a, too.

"Purply died," a little raggedy-haired girl reported, staring into the fish tank. "He became a fly," she said.

Like Hagen, I thought, remembering it all these years later. The way I thought he might be dead. Might as well be, now.

Gus came back down the hall. "I don't know where she got that," he said and handed Barf a Glad bag full of gray-brown mush-rooms.

"Maybe she's a Hindu," I said.

***

Back at our place, Barf and I were sorting piles of stems and caps when Ko showed up.

"You got 'em?" Ko asked when I opened the door.

Some shaggy-looking dude was with him.

I lifted my chin at the shaggy-looking dude and then looked back at Ko.

"Oh,"said Ko. "This is my bro, Greg. He's from Utah. He's cool."

I let them in and handed over Ko's share of the Glad bag. Ko cackled.

"How you want to do it, dude? Should we order a pizza?"

"I don't know, man. They work better on an empty stomach."

"But they taste like shit."

"That's what they grow in."

"You gotta just embrace it. I chew mine up, and put it between my cheek and gum like it's Skoal, but I don't spit," said Greg.

"Just chew 'em and swallow. On an empty stomach. It'll get into your blood stream better," one of us said.

***

"You feel anything?"

"These things are duds."

"It's cool how much you can drink shroomin'."

The music sounded differently depending on which way I tilted my head.

Yamaha showed up, face the color of a half-ripe tomato, with a bag of weed. He gobbled down his share and settled in on a couch. "Yo, Jizz, how was your camping trip at the Joshua Tree?"

"Epic. Like you stepped off a spaceship on some Twilight Zone planet. The trees are a trip. How long they've been there—you can totally tell they're alive, man. Each one's got its own pose and personality...tortured...exalting. It's a trip. It's like a forest in the

177

desert, but not like a dense forest. The trees are spaced out, like stars—but out there the stars aren't spaced out; there are so many, the sky's light as it is dark. But the best part is the rocks—"

"We should go there right now."

"Yeah! Let's take the spaceship to the Twilight Zone!"

"Who can drive?"

"I can drive, dude. These mushrooms didn't do shit. We can't take my Camaro, though," said Ko.

I shrugged. "We can take the Buick."

"Let's light a fire at the Joshua Tree!" Yamaha shouted.

"We'll need more beer."

We drove to the liquor store and bought four cases of cheap beer for the four of us.

"You think ninety-six beers is enough?"

"I hope so. I'm outta dough."

"Me, too."

"What's that smell?"

"My friend threw a butt out the window on the freeway, and it blew in the back window and set the upholstery on fire." I let out a whoop and cracked open a beer in front of the gas station mini-mart.

"This is insane," Greg said. "We're all drunk and stoned and freakin' on mushrooms, man. We should be chilling on the beach, dude, not driving the freeway two hundred miles to sit out in the desert. We're gonna get busted or killed or kill someone. Why?"

My muscles were buzzing and my eyes felt big. The world seemed to pause. They were all looking at me. I looked back at each one of them and said, "Why do people climb Everest? That's why, dude. Why put men on the moon? I don't know. But whatever that reason is, that's why. To prove it can be done. We can give you a ride back, though, and you can sit on the couch and watch *Friends* if you want."

"I'll walk." He was already sidling away.

I shrugged. "Let's go."

***

It was quiet in the car. I felt reason slipping away. I had to keep it going. "So the rocks are these crazy jumbles of boulders upon boulders upon boulders. The pamphlet the rangers give you says the place is called Joshua Tree because the Mormon pioneers thought the trees look like the out-stretched arms of the prophet Joshua. But I think it's called Joshua Tree because the boulders look like the ruins of Jericho. I read about Joshua in the Bible. The Bible says Joshua rode around the city and blew down the walls with a trumpet—"

"Yeah, man!" Yamaha yelled from the back seat.

"—and God stopped the sun so Joshua would have more time. Trip out on that. But geologists say the boulders were under hills, and what happened was the soil all around the boulders eroded away over time, leaving these giant jumbles of rock."

Like memory, I thought sitting in the stands tonight. Like the past. Like this story.

"Hagen and I got there around sundown. The light on the rocks looked like movie lighting, man, the clarity seemed supernatural. And the color faded, and it was like the impression of reality." I really did used to talk like that.

"The impression of reality!" Yamaha sounded like he was at a meeting of revivalists.

"And then the stars come out. One at a time. You look and you see one and then another, and then you look deeper, and you see more, and then it gets dark, and they're everywhere, and they come right down to the horizon."

"As light as it is dark!" sang Yamaha.

"Yeah. We built a fire and warmed some cans of chili and drank beer, and I swear to God, coyotes came and sat just beyond the ring of firelight and smiled and listened to our stories and said stuff in coyote that we didn't really understand. Hand me another beer, willya?"

"Where are we?"

"Chino."

"If we're gonna light a fire, we need firewood."

"Huh."

We got off the freeway somewhere and found a supermarket with cords of firewood stacked out in front. We pulled up, popped the trunk, got out, threw in a few bundles, and drove off without paying.

"Is that a cop?"

"What?"

"Just as we turned the corner, I thought I saw a cop pull into the parking lot."

"Don't worry." I cackled. "I'll talk to 'em. I bet I could talk 'em into letting me be sheriff for the day right now."

"Dude, I don't want to drive anymore," said Ko

"Pull over. I'll drive," I said.

Ko pulled off at some random exit and made a right and a left and went a little ways and made another right, and there was a parking lot on the back side of some high school near the visitors' stands at the football field. He stopped the car.

"I gotta piss," Barf said. "Lemme out." He stumbled over his seatbelt trying to get out of the car and splashed beer on his face and shirt. "Aw, heck!" he said and we all exploded in laughter.

"Heck?" This was the funniest thing anyone had ever said in the history of the world. "Heck? What is heck?"

"Must be some combination of hell and fuck."

Insanely, joyously, helplessly, we laughed. Our laughter carried us out to the football field where we tackled each other and lay on the grass and mumbled revelations, and shrieked and wailed and loved all creation.

I walked up into the stands and swigged the rest of my beer and belched loudly. Yamaha sat near me, and then Barf and Ko were sitting there in the dark, too.

That was how we ended up in the grandstands where eighteen years later I found myself sitting again.

"So Hagen and I are there to go rock climbing, right?" I said to the guys while we sat there in the dark. "And we drive around the place for like two hours looking for the highest jumble of boulders we can find. We're sipping beers and going down all these different dirt roads and we see this mountain of boulders must be half mile away and near a thousand feet high, with one boulder at the peak sticking up just perfect, so we stop, and we haven't seen any other cars the whole time, so you know, we're out there. And we have another beer, and walk across the desert to the bottom of this mountainous jumble of boulders and start climbing hand over hand, no equipment, and an hour later, we're still climbing and not even halfway to the top. It was way bigger than it looked, and the boulders are all shapes and slanted in all directions, and puzzling the way to go ain't easy. And suddenly

180

my night of chili and cheap beer is coming back to me, and I gotta crap, but I ain't got no toilet paper, so I gotta climb with my sphinx clenched, which is hard to do scaling a mountain of boulders.

"Anyway, we get to the top, or almost; all we gotta do is get to the top of that last big-ass boulder, only it's like sixty feet tall. Hagen thinks we should go up the left side, and I see a perfect ledge like a sidewalk sloping up around the right side. So we say, 'All right, race ya to the top." I made it about halfway up this rock when the ledge I'm on starts narrowing until it's less than a foot wide and drops off however many hundred feet it is to where, if I fall, I'll be dashed to bits on the jagged rocks below. But I keep creeping around, and it looks like if I can just get up and over about another ten feet, I'll be free and clear, except the ledge has narrowed to a toehold, and the rock I'm facing is rounded like the belly of a pregnant fifty-foot woman. If I can just get over the round part, it'll be easy to scramble to the top. So, I like humped halfway up the round part, using my elbows and knees as much as my hands and feet to wriggle up, and soon there's nothing under my feet. I couldn't see below me because of the roundness of the rock, and I started to get scared, like panicky scared. I only needed to shimmy up a few more feet, but I was afraid if I moved again, I'd slide back, miss the toehold and fucking die! And the worst thing was like I was just thinking that all I would be to anyone anymore was some dumb-ass who fell rock climbing at Joshua Tree. So I just lay paralyzed for God knows how long, afraid to go up, and afraid to go down.

"The warm rock pressing against my face, the breeze blowing my hair, I actually got pretty comfortable. My breathing got all deep, and I might have fallen asleep, but I had to take a crap so bad, and my need to crap, and to crap not in my pants, overcame my fear of dying. I slid back down the round rock, slowly, slowly, searching with my toes, feeling, feeling, and then I was sliding out of control, fast—I couldn't slow myself, and I thought I was a dead man, but my toes hit the ledge, and I was able to stop myself and sidle back down the ledge the way I had come.

"So I went up the way Hagen had gone, but he wasn't at the top when I got there. The sky circled me. Far below, the car sat like a tiny toy. I called his name and the sound of the wind buffeted by ears. I looked down the other side of the mountain at nothing but boulders

181

and crevices. I looked over all the edges calling and calling, but nothing. I figured he got sick of waiting for me and must've gone back. So I start back down, sphincter clenched, figuring in about another minute I'd have to crap right there and use my underwear for toilet paper and free-ball it the rest of the way, when I spot a snakebite kit just sitting there on a rock like a gift from God. I open it and it's got gauze in it. Yee-haw. I barely got my drawers down before chili and Meister Brau came blowing out like a brass band playing at the eruption of Vesuvius, but I got to keep my drawers.

"Anyway, I climbed all the way down the mountain of boulders and hiked back across the desert to the car, but Hagen wasn't there. The car was locked, and he had the keys, and it was getting hotter and hotter. After a couple of hours, I thought he might be hurt up there. I hiked back across the desert and climbed the mountain of boulders again yelling his name every minute. I climbed about halfway down the other side looking for him, and he ain't anywhere. Back to the car. What am I going to do? Hike along the road, try to find a ranger? Get a rescue team? I don't know. I sat there in what shade of the car there was and waited, thirsty, and hungry. It got dark, and I guessed I was going to be spending the night on the hood of the car. I'd go at first light to look for help. I'd have to break a window to get water out of the car. And I was scared, man. What if Hagen was dead? What if coyotes were gnawing on him? Will I be blamed? I was trying to sleep, but it wasn't happening, just all these terrible thoughts. And then, out of the night, here comes Hagen.

"Dude!"

"What the heck!"

"I don't know, man," he said. "I got to the top and you never came, so I thought you must have beaten me and gone back, so I went down, but I must've gone the wrong way. I came down in some valley on the other side. It's like a maze back in there. I've been walking all day and night. I finally came to this road; I didn't know if it was the right road or not, or which way to go on it, or anything, but I just kept walking on it, and here I am now."

"What the huck," Barf said, "We gonna see this place or sit around talking about it all night? He crushed his beer can and let it fall under the stands.

I looked down two decades later to see if it might still be

there, but it wasn't.

"Yeah, let's get the full out of here," I said.

I drove. The world was breathing. I could feel the chest of the universe expanding and contracting. The world was full of chaos and motion, but through it all was a little tunnel of physical consistency through which I could drive if I kept my eyes on the road and my hands upon the wheel. The sign for the monument materialized along the side of the road, and I steered onto the ramp that banked over the freeway and into the dark desert. The wind howled and pushed the car, forcing me to yank the wheel against it.

"Man, how can you drive right now?" Barf said. "I'm seeing the stars rain on the windshield, and my fingers are snakes."

I felt heroic. I was able to do it. I was the leader. When we had tried to decide for sure whether or not to drive out to Joshua Tree, Barf said, "You're the one who has to decide. You're the leader." And here it was true. I was the man making it all happen.

We stopped somewhere surrounded by darkness. The wind was screaming and cold. We got out and were exultant as if we'd achieved some mystical mastery of the universe in our ability to get there.

The sense of triumph lasted five minutes before everyone wanted to get back in the car because of the cold wind.

Yamaha said, "I thought we were going to light a fire at the Joshua Tree."

"We don't have any paper to kindle a fire."

"Use your journal," one of them said to me.

"Screw that."

"We can't light the fire without it. That's why we came. To light a fire at the Joshua Tree."

"We're not burning my journal."

"What have you got in there that's so important?"

An unanswerable question. *My life? Nothing?* It was how I remembered. It was for the sublime sensation of creation passing through me.

Yamaha snatched the journal out from under my arm. I lunged for it, and he tossed it to Barf. I gave Barf what I thought was an imploring look in the dark. "Come on, dude."

"Jizz, were freezing, man." He tore out a handful of pages,

183

and the wind immediately ripped them from his hand and scattered them to the desert night. "Oops." He tore out some more pages and tossed the rest of the book back to me.

"You could have at least tried to get some with no writing on them."

"You could have done that in the first place."

They stuffed the paper in amongst the stolen logs and tried to get a fire started, but even when we were able to keep a match lit for a few seconds, the paper burned into embers and blew away before the wood caught.

"It was all shit anyway," I can remember muttering.

Soon the last of the matches was gone. Huddled against each other in the car, the breathing of the guys became rhythmic and the wind groaned around us and shook, and the sensation of creation came. In the remnants of the notebook I scratched words to try to capture it, writing all over the page because I couldn't see the ruled lines in the dark, which, just like everything else, seemed to mean something. As the light came up in the East, it was like the coming of the future, and out the window to the West, the past faded away, while in the car the present always and never existed; now was always ending, always becoming the past, always becoming the future, perpetually obliterated, never over, always happening, inescapable; the present is ever the past which can only be remembered in the future. With a brain full of psilocybin, this had been a stunning revelation, a miracle we take for granted every day. I scribbled and scribbled. Yes, yes. The primal truths became apparent. I wrote them all down. *Yes, yes, I have something here*, I thought.

\*\*\*

The wind had stopped gusting. The guys snored uncomfortably. I heard exasperation in their breaths, dissatisfaction, a sense of having been swindled. I forced my eyes to stay shut, forced my breathing to slow, but it was nothing like sleep. My neurons fired randomly, bouncing my legs, shooting off voices in my mind that spoke non-sequitur sentence fragments. The future didn't come for a long time. When it did, it came with a tapping that didn't seem to be coming from inside my head. I didn't want to open my eyes, but the tapping persisted, along with a voice that croaked like a raven's, and also did not seem to be coming from inside my head. "Wake up," it said. I opened my eyes. An old woman was tapping the window with a flashlight in the gray morning, right by my head. She wore a ranger hat. I opened the door, and stood unsteadily out of the car, surrounded by beer cans, urine stains, and torn, half-burned journal pages.

"This is disgusting," she said.

I bleated apologies, yes ma'am-ing, and no ma'am-ing, as she varied her expressions of disdain. I groveled about collecting the cans and pages of scrawl that tried to mean something. She said we owed ten dollars for the entrance fee. I froze holding armloads of garbage, no trashcan anywhere. Money. I tried to open the car door without dropping the cans and journal pages, dropped most of them anyway, and threw the rest in on top of the bodies in the back seat. "Wake up. The ranger's here." Nobody moved. "Guys." I looked at the ranger lamely and searched my pockets. I found four wadded ones. "Barf, Ko, Yamaha, wake up and pay the ranger." I searched the ranger's weather-beaten face for some sign of understanding and found nothing. "Here." I gave her the four dollars and my license and a credit card. "We'll get this place cleaned up, and go into town and get cash. Then we'll come to the ranger station and pay you, and you can hold on to this stuff so you know we'll come."

"The kiosk at the main entrance, up that way," she said and got into a green pick-up truck and bounced down the road. I started the car and drove toward town for money.

*** 

We headed home after paying the ranger. If going south on Highway 215, it hits the 91 west without having to change freeways, so coming westbound on the 60, I took the 215 south expecting to hit the 91 back to Newport Beach, but it never becomes the 91, because, as I learned years later, the 215 is disconnected for several miles by the 60. We were halfway to San Diego.

The guys took turns blowing air out of their mouths, grunts that said they wanted to be out of the car, away from this mad foolishness. "I don't understand it," I kept saying. "It doesn't make any sense. The 215 is supposed to turn into the 91. Did the whole world

185

change?"

It was Barf that ended up getting us home after I had become despondent with incomprehension. In the passenger seat, in the sober light of day, I looked through the jagged remains of my journal and found the primal truths I'd written at dawn were little more than gibberish.

All gone now, I thought, sitting twenty years in the future. Barf, Ko, and Yamaha have all disappeared from the present, obliterated by car payments, insurance premiums, legal fees, marriage counseling, alarm clocks. Hagen might as well have died that day, because he doesn't exist anymore, as far as I know. And I'm not sure how or when, but the past definitely passes. I stood up, descended the grandstands, and walked to work.

# Contributor Biographies

**Cynthia Anderson** lives in the high desert near Joshua Tree National Park. Her poems have appeared in numerous journals and won several awards. Her latest book is *In the Mojave* (Pencil Cholla Press, 2011). She is co-editor of *A Bird Black as the Sun: California Poets on Crows & Ravens* (Green Poet Press, 2011). Both books are available at amazon.com. She blogs about the high desert at http://cynthiashidesertblog.blogspot.com

**Jennifer L. Bielman** is a writer, book blogger, and social media consultant. She is also a member of the Inland Empire California Writers Club. Though she has a B.S. in Business Administration from the University of Redlands, writing is her passion. She is currently working on her first urban fantasy novel. You can often find her staying up late to finish a good book, admiring her ridiculously long hair, and laughing way too loudly. She loves dogs but a stray cat has taken residence in her backyard and has slowly assimilated herself into the family. She's been aptly named Cat.

**t.s. bennett** used up the good teachers at USC and dropped out. self-published two thin books of poetry in the 1990s. "burr under harness" and "crossing the rubicon". wrote and published a book in 2008, titled *confessions of the antichrist.* it is an anti-autobiographical, semi historical reality documentary.the antichrist has always been snotty and has yet to be defined by the church or state.

**Pierce J Boulet**, born and reared in the Inland Empire, returned to roost several years ago after stints in Northern CA, Oregon, Ojai and Los Angeles. She is currently enrolled in the UCLA Extension Creative Writing program and is participating in her third session of Inlandia's Riverside writing workshop. She has worked for the last 32 years, among other projects and careers, as a sign language interpreter.

**Celena Diana Bumpus** was born and raised in Seattle, Washington. After visiting her grandparents in the Inland Empire every Christmas and summer break for years, she and her mother relocated to San Bernardino, California, when she was nine years old. Her grandparents needed assistance with their care. During high school, she moved away from the Inland Empire to go to high school in other states. Returning to San Bernardino, she graduated from high school, completed college at San Bernardino Valley College (SBVC) with an Associates Degree in Liberal Arts in 1991, then transferred to the University of California, Riverside, receiving a certificate from UCR Extension in Advanced Alcohol and Other Drugs of Abuse in 1993. She has worked in the Inland Empire as a city, county, state and Department of Defense employee, excelling in program design and auditing for both non-profit, for-profit and government organizations.

**Mike Cluff** is a full-time English, critical thinking and creative writing professor at Norco (Community) College in Southern California. He is currently putting the final touches on his tenth poetry book called *The Initial Napoleon*.

**Dr. Carlos E. Cortés** is professor emeritus of history at the University of California, Riverside. His most recent book is his autobiography, *Rose Hill: An Intermarriage before Its Time* (Berkeley, CA: Heyday, 2012). Other books include *The Children Are Watching: How the Media Teach about Diversity and The Making—and Remaking—of a Multiculturalist*, published by Teachers College Press. Cortés is general editor of the forthcoming *Multicultural America: A Multimedia Encyclopedia* (Sage, 2013), scholar-in-residence with Univision Communications, and creative/cultural advisor for Nickelodeon's Peabody-award-winning children's television series, *Dora the Explorer*, and its sequel, *Go, Diego, Go!*, for which he received the 2009 NAACP Image Award. He also travels the country performing his one-person autobiographical play, *A Conversation with Alana: One Boy's Multicultural Rite of Passage*, while he co-wrote the book and lyrics for the musical, *We Are Not Alone: Tomás Rivera—A Musical Narrative*, which premiered in 2011.

**Laurel V. Cortés**: At 17, I went to Mexico City alone to attend the University of Mexico. The experience changed my life and, after majoring in Spanish and minoring in Comparative Literature at San Diego State University, I worked for 28 years at the University of California, Riverside, in—guess what?—the Department of Literatures and Languages. The job perfectly suited my interests, and it's fun now to do a bit of writing on my own.

**Larry J. Dunlap** was born in Brooklyn New York, raised in Indianapolis, Indiana, and continues to mature in California. He worked for many years in the music, film and video industry including founding the first cable television network to use digital broadcasting. He has developed online games, and been a technical writer and training author for Fortune 100 companies. He writes fiction and non-fiction from his home in Southern California where he lives with his wife, Laurie, and Chili Dog. He is currently working on a book-length memoir, *Look Back in Love - My Life as A Naked Car Thief*. http://ANakedCarThief.com

**Myra Dutton** is the author of *Healing Ground: A Visionary Union of Earth and Spirit*, which was a 2004 Narcissus Book Award finalist, recognized as one of 2003's "Top Ten Books" by *Shutterbug Magazine*, and was a 2006's "Ten Books We Love" selection by *Inland Empire Magazine*. She was interviewed on NPR's *Environmental Directions Radio* in October 2005 and was a featured poet on the *Tree of Life* special for the PBS Emmy Award-winning program, *Eco-News* in December 2006. She jointly leads the Idyllwild Inlandia Institute Creative Writing Workshop with Jean Waggoner.

**Amy Floyd** has been a member of the Inlandia Writing Group since its beginning. She has published short fiction in the *Slouching Toward Mt. Rubidoux Manner* chapbooks, the Inlandia anthologies and *Phantom Seed*. Her artwork was recently published in the book *A Bird As Black As the Sun*. She continues to write short fiction and publishes electronically with her story collection *Do Serial Killers Smile At Their Victims?* available for sale through Amazon. Be sure to check out her latest project on http://plotroach.blogspot.com/.

**Françoise Frigola** writes spontaneously, often on current social issues. French-born Françoise is a regular attendee of the Idyllwild Inlandia workshop. She is also an internationally exhibited and collected artist and a computer consultant.

**David Calvin Gogerty** is an economist with a Stanford bachelor's and master's whose professional work is for private clients on problems of risk analysis. He is a co-author of articles in peer-reviewed journals in economics and operations research. He and his wife live in Idyllwild.

**Michelle Gonzalez** earned her BA in English from the University of California, Riverside. She also received her teaching credential from University of Phoenix and MFA in creative writing from National University. For the past 29 years she has lived in Riverside and has no plans on leaving the Inland Empire. Her poems have been published in National University's literary magazine and other local magazines. Michelle plans to publish her first book of poems soon as well as continuing her teaching career. Michelle Gonzalez has been a participant in the Riverside workshop since 2009.

**Marie Griffiths**, a former registered nurse and English instructor, is retired and lives with her husband, Garry, in Fontana, California. A chronic "late bloomer," Marie began a liberal arts education in middle age, ultimately earning a Ph.D. from UCR in 1999. Still a neophyte in the realm of creative writing, she continues to hone her craft by composing short stories and poems. She is a proud member of the Inland Empire branch of the California Writers' Club.

**Joan Koerper**, Ph.D., has published creative nonfiction/memoir, poetry, fiction, and nonfiction. These embrace her book, *Singing over the Bones, Pottery and Writing as Expressions of Soul as Artist* (UMI, 2004) and works appearing in *Sacred Fire* (Adams Media), *Moondance*, *Clay Times*, *The Single Parent*, newspapers, research housed in libraries and Inlandia supported publications among other venues. Productions for adults and children include: radio scripts for PBS, video and audiotape scripts, and a Chautuaqua-style one-woman play. Active with Paws for Literacy, Joan and her dog Sage have completed their third chapter book in the series, *The Adventures of Sage, The Super Service Dog*. Joan has taught over thirty undergraduate and graduate classes at four universities.

**Mick Lynch** has spent his whole life in and around the entertainment business. He has worked professionally as an Irish musician, actor, writer, film editor and director. After retiring from his Hollywood duties as an episodic television director and editor, Mick moved to Idyllwild, California, where he has written and performed a radio style ensemble reading, *The Adventures Of Dan*, and two one-man shows: *Out of the Pine* and *Forever the Stranger*. He has also sung and played with Two Micks and a Chick, a local Irish band which he helped form. As of now Lynch says that he will continue to write and interpret his works both dramatically and musically as the muse moves.

**Krystal B. Moon** is a nineteen-year-old short story writer from San Bernardino, California. She has been writing for the last four years and focuses on romance, tragedy and drama. Krystal aspires to one day publish a collection of her short stories.

**Richard M. Mozeleski** is a retired landscape designer. He has been married to his wife Diane for 22 years, and is the father of Ian Mozeleski, a college basketball player. Richard has coached local basketball and baseball players for the past decade and took up writing and theater after moving to Idyllwild. Richard also does a ministry feeding the homeless.

**T Qi "Hillbilly Mystic" AKA Teresa Halliburton** is a Shaolin Qi Specialist, from Tennessee. T Qi's work includes "Limitless" and "Stone Panther" published in *Idyll Wild Words,* collaborative works "Orgasm" and "B.I.T.E. M.E." for *The Poet's Eye-The Artist Tongue*, visual arts show; and for *Verbal Moonshine* readings at the Santa Cruz Mountains Art Center. She sang with U.N.L.V.; and on *Winter Calls*, a Local Color CD. Book T Qi @ 831-247-4784 More available soon at www.108poems.com.

**Timothy Perez** is a graduate of Cal State Long Beach's MFA program. He works in Corona, lives in Riverside, and writes wherever and whenever.

**Linda Rhoades** has a bachelor of science degree in communications from Cal Poly Pomona and a certificate in Fiction Writing from the University of California Riverside Extension. When her children had the good grace to become self-reliant, she began to write full time. Her short story, "Lunch with Paula Stone" was published in the online magazine *Cynic* (cynicmag.com) in October 2011. An amateur photographer, Linda's work will be published in the Fall issue of the online journal *Wild Lemon Project* (wildlemonproject.org) in October 2012. "Coco" is Linda's first submission to the Inlandia Anthology. She is writing her first novel.

**Jacqueline Mantz Rodriguez** was born in Great Falls, Montana but immigrated to the Inland Empire as a young child growing up in Ontario, California. She resides in Palm Springs and is a special education teacher at Palm Springs High. She is editing her novella, *The Long Unforgiving Road*. Jacqueline received her B.A. in literature and creative writing from Cal State San Bernardino and her master's degree and teaching credentials from National University. Jacqueline's loves are her husband Joe and her Boston Terrier Elizabeth Barrett Browning.

**Marsha Schuh** is an instructor at California State University, San Bernardino and a lifelong lover of learning, teaching, and writing. She received her BA in English from Willamette University a lifetime ago and returned to school in1997 to earn an MBA from the University of La Verne and later, an MA in English Composition and an MFA in poetry from CSUSB. That makes her a MBAMAMFA. Marsha's MFA thesis, *Tracings in Crystal*, explores the meaning of place, family, memory, and curiosity from her perspective as a second-generation Swedish-American transplanted to California. Marsha and her husband have lived in Ontario for 37 years. Her poems and essays have appeared in *Pacific Review*, *Ghost Town*, *Badlands*, *Sand Canyon Review*, and *Meat*. She also co-authored a college textbook, *Computer Networking*, published in 2003 by Prentice-Hall. It's now outdated, but she's still proud of her chapters on LANs, the Internet, and an appendix on converting binary to decimal. Perhaps she'll turn them into poetry one fine day. Until then, she is working on a colle tion of poems about the streets of Ontario.

Since moving to Palm Desert several years ago, **Tami Sigurdson** has been capturing the striking contrasts of the flora and fauna of the desert and its unique beauty with her photography, which she continues to further her interests in. Coupled with the images she creates, she most enjoys putting pen to paper and spends her spare time writing poetry and short stories reflecting on her keen interest in social studies and life experiences.

**Joy Sikorski**, M.A. is an award-winning film composer, published author (*Singing Through Life With Your Mouth Closed, Los Angeles Family Magazine, Inlandia Anthology 2011*), founder of SingBabySing® and Singing Mastermind™, co-composer/lyricist for *Gathering Blue*, a new musical based on Newberry Award-winning author Lois Lowry's book by the same title. Joy has written incidental music for the South Coast Repertory Theatre's commissioned musical, *Wind in the Willows*, has appeared on television and is known for her unique performance genre, "Impropera-Music of the Moment," in which she concurrently creates music and lyrics while singing and playing the piano before live audiences. She is currently working on several book projects and voice-training programs. In other news, she bore and raised three children in a log cabin she helped to build in Alaska.

**Mike Sleboda** earned his Associate of Arts from Riverside City College and his BA in communications from Cal. State San Bernardino. A long time member of the Riverside Creative Writing Workshop, he has been published in both *Slouching Towards Mt. Rubidoux Manor* and the Inlandia anthologies. He volunteers for the Inlandia Institute and is an avid car enthusiast/mechanic. He enjoys drawing/sketching and building model cars and plans to pursue a career in the film industry.

**Bob Smith** identifies the two threads of continuity in his life as I-15— he grew up in San Diego County, but spent his adult life in Las Vegas, then Ogden, Utah – and writing – technical, bureaucratic, journalistic, creative, you name it.. With a Ph.D. from Berkeley, his day jobs were chemistry professor and university executive. Long since retired, he is now a local historian and newspaper columnist. His nature essays have appeared in *Weber: The Contemporary West* (formerly *Weber Studies*) and won the annual Utah Original Writing Competition.

**Kelly Smith** writes picture books and humor/photography. She loves to write a variety of picture books which include fantasy, humor, and realistic fiction with a Christian theme. She lives in Corona, California, with her husband Dan, two beautiful daughters Sarah and Heather, three cats and a dog. She has worked in special education for twelve years and was a professional clown for more than a decade. It is her gift to make people laugh that inspired her to write humor/pho-tography.

**Gillian Spedding** is a writer and visual artist living in the desert.

**Diana Twiss** comes from a long line of natural storytellers. As a child, her favorite pastime was to sit under the table as the adults shared sto-ries above, and the other kids played outside. She is most intrigued and delighted by the details of everyday life. This is the fabric of her poems. She is a new mama, a happy wife, and the careful guardian of some chickens, dogs and turtles. When she isn't writing, she's usually got her toes in the mud. This is her first publication--unless you count a brilliant poem published at age thirteen in a synchronized swimming magazine, *USA Synchro Magazine* (unfortunately, they don't offer back-issues).

**Jean Waggoner** teaches English/English as a Second Language at several community colleges in Riverside County. She serves as one of Inlandia's Idyllwild workshop leaders with Myra Dutton and as an officer of the California Part-time Faculty Association. Her work has appeared in national and regional publications, including peer-reviewed journals and poetry blogs. In 2011 Jean and co-author

Douglas Snow published *The Freeway Flier and the Life of the Mind*, a book that explores the challenges of creating while teaching.

**Mae Wagner** currently writes a column for her home town newspaper in Hettinger, North Dakota. When the *Press-Enterprise* was locally owned, several of her columns were published on the op-ed page and she has also written for the Riverside Chamber of Commerce and the Chino Champion. She has been a member of the Inlandia Riverside Creative Writing Workshop since its beginning and enjoys sharing her memories of the Inland Empire in the workshop's publications. Mother of three, grandmother of seven and great-grandmother of two, she lives in Redlands with her husband, Alex, and dog, Sophie.

**Kathryn Wilkens** began writing for publication in 2000. Several of her travel articles have appeared in *The Los Angeles Times*. She has written essays and articles for *Writers' Journal, Personal Journaling, Verbatim* and *The Christian Science Monitor*. Four of her essays have appeared in anthologies, most recently *Writers and Their Notebooks* (South Carolina Press, 2009). She lives a short drive from the Ovitt Family Community Library in Ontario where she has enjoyed Cati Porter's Inlandia workshop.

**Janis Young** is a native of Riverside whose family has lived there for four generations. As a librarian at the Ovitt Family Community Library in Ontario, she has an abiding love of books and all things literary. She believes nothing is as fine as good poetry or a Lawrence Durrell novel. In addition to participating in the Inlandia Writing Workshop with Cati Porter, Janis is also a member of the Inland Empire California Writers Club. She has lived in various parts of the country, and she believes that regional differences as well as social climate have a great deal to do with creativity. In her opinion, the region most conducive to successful writing in the U.S. is the South. Janis looks forward to meeting and learning from other aspiring writers.

**J. Ladd Zorn, Jr.**, B.A., University of California, Irvine, Certificate in Fiction Writing, U. C. Riverside, teaches on the edge of the Southern California megalopolis and the Mojave Desert.His fiction has appeared in the literary journal *Phantom Seeds* (Heyday Books) and the 2011 Writing From Inlandia.He is seeking a publisher for his novel, *Car Trouble*, and is at work on his second book-length effort, *Maineiac*, based upon a cross-country road trip to Maine where he worked as a lobsterman. Mr. Zorn is a former *Jeopardy!* Champion.

## About the Inlandia Institute

**The Inlandia Institute** is a regional non-profit literary center. We seek to bring focus to the richness of the literary enterprise that has existed in this region for ages. The mission of the Inlandia Institute is to recognize, support and expand literary activity in all of its forms through community programs in the Inland Empire, thereby deepening people's awareness, understanding, and appreciation of this unique, complex and creatively vibrant region.

The Institute publishes high quality regional writing in print and electronic form including books published in partnership with Heyday under the Inlandia Institute imprint as well as: *Writing From Inlandia: Work of the Inlandia Creative Writing Workshops*; the online literary journal, *Inlandia: A Literary Journey; and*, starting the winter of 2011, books directly under the Inandia imprint, including *Dos Chiles / Two Chilies*, a children's chapter book by Julianna Cruz.

Inlandia presents free public literary programming featuring authors who live in, work in, and/or write about Inland Southern California. We also provide Creative Literacy Programs for children and youth and hold creative writing workshops for teens and adults.

To learn more about the Inlandia Institute please visit our website at InlandiaInstitute.org.

# OTHER INLANDIA PUBLICATIONS

INLANDIA ELECTRONIC PUBLICATIONS

*Inlandia: A Literary Journey*, an on-line journal
Edited by Cati Porter

*Inlandia: A Literary Journey Through California's Inland Empire*
Audio Guide
Moderated by Gayle Brandeis


OTHER INLANDIA IMPRINT PUBLICATIONS

*2011 Writing from Inlandia*
Editorial Board

*Dos Chiles / Two Chilies*
Julianna Cruz


INLANDIA IMPRINT BOOKS FROM HEYDAY

*Backyard Birds of the Inland Empire*
Sheila N. Kee

*Dream Street*
Douglas F. McCulloh, forward by D.J. Waldie

*Inlandia:A Literary Journey Through California's Inland Empire*
Edited by Gayle Wattawa, introduction by Susan Straight

*No Place for a Puritan: The Literature of California's Deserts*
Edited by Ruth Nolan

*Rose Hill*
Carlos Cortez

Expected 2013
*Vital Signs*
Juan Delgado & Thomas McGovern

www.ingramcontent.com/pod-product-compliance
Lightning Source LLC
Chambersburg PA
CBHW051827090426

42736CB00011B/1691